paradox

of the

water
bearer

leilani mañulu

First paperback edition July 2021
ISBN 978-1-7372639-0-6 (print)
ISBN 978-1-7372639-1-3 (ebook)

www.shamanleilani.com

For my ancestors, guides, and loved ones lost. Thank you for always seeing me with such clarity and for continually reminding me of my strength, courage, and valor.

ACKNOWLEDGMENTS

This book would not be possible without my family and soul connections.

My son: James Finley. You are my heart, my motivation, my reason for breathing. I love you with every fiber of my being, and I hope to always make you proud.

My siblings: Kristine, Jacqueline, Greg, and Lawrence. You are my heart, and I move through this life knowing exactly who I am because I see myself in you. We belong to one another and I love you always.

My parents: Zane, Edwin, and Nelia. Mom, thank you for raising me to be a strong woman who knows exactly how to use my voice. Dad, thank you for always believing in me and allowing me to be a part of your healing journey. Nanay, your unconditional love has been a staple in my life. I could not be who I am without you all. You are so important to me.

My nieces and nephew: Ky, Nat, Stella, Quinn, Kendrick, and Hollis. Thank you for reminding me every day how to live in the present moment and truly experience joy, love, and gratitude.

My spiritual and chosen family: Jonathan G., Kendall, Craig, Mike T., Anika, Meesa, Josette, Courtney, Arham, Tarrah, Jill, Nate, Adana, Jess L., Kailei, Dianna, Jen, Jess C., Bill, Glenn, Chrissy E., Ben, Chrissy Z., Emma, Cait, Raegan, Zan, Liz, Jonathan M., Myra, and Malik. Thank you for always reminding me of the power of my angel wings and giving me the courage to tell my story.

My writing coach: Sage. You've pulled me out of the depths of my paralysis and the disbelief in my abilities time and time and time again. Thank you for always holding up the light when I couldn't see it myself. I'm so grateful for you and how you see me.

PROLOGUE:

BEFORE THE BEGINNING

Fitzsimmons, Colorado
March 1989

Something about the smell of roses brings me back to my innocence. A time when I could indulge my senses without having to do so with caution, as if it were possible to cross a threshold when being in my body would be too much. Like slowly tiptoeing toward the edge of a cliff to carefully peer over the side, only to find the ground beneath beginning to crumble and suddenly give way. There is something about that fear, the fear of losing my footing and slipping away from reality, as I begin to access something that is buried down below my skin. Below my flesh.

The smell of roses takes me back to a time when I did not have to worry about losing my footing. When I could dance and frolic in the giant field near our small apartment with my sisters, being so fully in my body that I felt as though I was one with the Earth beneath my bare feet. I could run and jump and feel every sensation, every emotion, without caution. Without fear of losing what I've so carefully built. This artfully curated exterior. This gross misrepresentation.

I'm still not sure why the roses represent this for me. When I was a young child, we never had rose bushes, or any garden of our own, for that matter. We lived in military housing, and my mother had exactly three tomato plants that were planted right outside our back door, but we didn't have our own yard or anything to distinguish our home from any other family's home.

My mother would water these three tomato plants and drone on and on about how she was sure that the dog that belonged to the family three units down was urinating on them.

"It's not good for the plants," she would say. "I better not catch that fucking dog pissing on my tomatoes."

I remember being surprised that tomatoes were green before they were red. Maybe it surprised me that what I saw after the tomatoes were plucked, delivered to the grocery store, then eventually tossed into our dinner on any given evening, was different than how the plants began. They had a story, an evolution. There was so much that happened before the moment those tomatoes made their way into my mother's spaghetti that formed that very plant. That very piece of food that eventually sustained us.

I remember thinking it was fascinating, that something as seemingly insignificant as a ripe tomato could have such an elaborate back story that I had no idea about, yet I consumed it so effortlessly, so voraciously, without taking the time to explore its origins. Its beginnings.

I do remember rose potpourri. My mother set out dried rose petals in our bathroom. The rose petals smelled lovely at first and eventually lost their scent. But they stayed in that bathroom. I remember staring at the rose petals, dust caked on their brittle bodies. I remember wondering what was the point of putting out the rose petals in the first place if they inevitably lost their scent and their usefulness. They weren't much to look at, and after about a week, they didn't smell anymore either. They just became this echo of something they once were.

I was 6 years old when that rose petal potpourri lost its scent. That was when my uncle came to stay with us in our small apartment to help with childcare.

What a funny word, childcare. So indiscriminate. Like, how do we know that the child is cared for? What criteria do we use? Are we checking in to make sure that care is happening? That these children are cared for? Who is to say? Who would know? Besides the child, of course.

But why would we ask a child if they feel cared for? Children should not have a voice, at least not in a military, Filipino, devout Catholic household. Children do as they are told. They are unremarkable. They serve a purpose. And they lie. They lie to get their way because children are selfish and self-serving.

Do children even deserve care?

What happens if a child doesn't get the care she herself thinks she deserves?

Does it even matter what she wants?

Is anybody listening?

Can you hear me? Can you see me?

I've lost myself again.

ARRIVAL

Renton, WA
Present Day, August 2020

I fidget with my pen, tapping it quickly against my black leather-bound journal, as I watch my computer slowly begin to bring up the virtual meeting room with Josette. The spinning circle signifying that the computer is slowly processing the command taunts me, painfully reminding me that I truly have no control over anything.

I glance down at the time on my computer: 6:31 PM.

Argh, late again! I scold myself silently as I continue to anxiously tap the pen against the black leather of the journal.

Finally, the meeting room pops up, and I see Josette. I glance down at the time: 6:32.

"Hi!" I say quickly, "I'm so sorry to be late. It's been a hectic evening. Work has been chaotic, and I had to do the dishes, and…"

I pause, yet continue to list the excuses in my mind, as Josette's face displays a soft, warm smile. She is a thin woman, likely late 30's or early 40's. Her skin is pale but slightly tan, her hair short and chestnut brown.

I glance at the little square displaying my own video and note the contrast in my energy in comparison to Josette's. My skin is a warm tan, and my dark hair falls past my shoulders, appearing frizzy and unkempt. I have dark circles under my eyes which seem to say, "Yes, I'm a working mom in the time of COVID-19," without actually saying anything at all. I look disheveled, like someone who is trying desperately to simply stay afloat. She looks like someone who just came from a relaxing day at the spa.

As I continue to take note of her energy, I begin to realize the calming effect she has on my spirit, and suddenly, I am completely present.

"I'm just so glad to finally meet you!" She says warmly. "I'm Josette."

I feel the tension in my shoulders and upper back release as I exhale and sink into my chair. It feels as though this is the first time I have felt my breath all day. *Have I been holding my breath this whole time?* I wonder to myself.

"I'm Leilani..." I reply, unsure of what to say next.

Josette and I had connected on social media a few days prior. I had seen a striking picture of her, her expression blank, but her vibrant blue eyes calling me toward her, as if asking to connect. I have always been drawn to people based on their eyes. I can see their intentions, fears, and hopes. I can tell how they are feeling and what they are holding energetically. However, in Josette's eyes, all I had seen was wonder. Expanse. I had seen a vast, blue ocean, and the answers to questions I had been asking myself since I was a child. I felt drawn to strike up a conversation with her via a private message, which led us to this very moment.

"So, tell me a little bit about yourself," Josette says before bringing her mug up to her lips with both hands and taking a sip.

"Well..." I begin, "As I mentioned in my message to you, in the last several months, I started communing pretty regularly with the spiritual realm. I have been getting messages through my intuition, messages for the people with which I am connecting at the time. My coaching clients, friends, colleagues, family. Sometimes it is someone I talk to regularly; often it is someone I barely know or haven't spoken with in a while. I can't explain it, but I think I'm here with you for a reason."

She puts her mug down on the desk, presses her lips together, and looks deeply into the camera, and suddenly, I feel as though she is looking straight into my soul. She takes a breath before gently asking, "And what reason is that?"

I consider her question, looking away from the screen while I contemplate what I have been seeking over the last several months, as if the answer would be somewhere else in the room, somewhere other than inside of me. After about a minute of silence, I look back at the computer screen. "To… understand," I reply simply. "I want to understand how I am supposed to use this gift, how to hone it, how to use it for the greatest good. And I think you may be able to help me."

She glances up for a few moments, seeming to digest what I have just said. "I see…" Her voice trails off a bit as if she is receiving information of her own, information perhaps that I am not privy to. "Well, let's just have a conversation and see where it takes us. I just ask that you are open during our time together. I'm going to ask you a series of questions, and I invite you to just drop down into your heart and your spirit to find the answer. Does that sound good to you?"

I drop my pen, which I had been gripping tightly, as I make the decision to not take notes; I don't want to micromanage this experience. This moment feels important, but I cannot reason in my mind why that may be. Then, the fear begins to creep in, as it often does for me… the fear of missing something important. I think to myself, *I hope she records this call so that I can…*

"Oh!" Josette says suddenly, snapping me back into the present moment, "I forgot to begin recording…"

A bit shocked, I chuckle nervously, "I just thought in my mind, 'I hope she records this so I can be present!'"

"Oh, wow! Yeah, you're powerful…" she says a bit absently, as she continues to search for the record function. I see a red dot begin to blink, signaling the beginning of the recording. "There we go!" she remarks.

I sense my brain begin to process quickly, which is what happens when I try to make sense of something that just doesn't make sense. This is something I am used to doing in my life. *You're powerful – what does that mean?* I shake off the thought as she looks back at me again, her warm eyes seeming to invite me forward.

"This is a soul seeker session, as I mentioned briefly in our previous exchange," she explains. "Often, clients connect with me to get clarity on their soul's work. I am going to ask you a series of questions; however, this is going to be a very fluid conversation. How does that sound?"

"That sounds great!" I say, feeling genuinely excited as my body begins to relax. I sense the anxiety melting away, being replaced with a feeling of awe and wonder, as if the Universe, or Source as I call my higher power, is guiding our exchange.

The conversation then becomes seamless, effortless. Her questions create a cocoon of safety and gently guide the conversation back and forth, like gentle and foamy waves on the Pacific Northwest coast. Each question allows the waves to push further up the shore, gently tugging at sand each time, shaping and molding the Earth into something that is the same, yet somehow incredibly different. Revolutionary. To the unknowing onlooker, the shore looks untouched. But to those who understand, those who are true seers, the grains of sand move into something completely different with each wave.

Before I even realize it, the conversation begins to come to an end. *Wow, where did the time go?* I ask myself. A voice suddenly enters my mind: *Time doesn't exist.*

The voice is not mine and it catches me off guard. *Time doesn't exist? What does that even mean?* I think to myself, asking whomever just provided that information to me. I listen intently for a response. Nothing.

I shake my head in an attempt to brush it off, refocusing my attention on Josette, who has begun to take on an ethereal energy. *Something very important is happening. Right here, right now.* It feels important and peaceful all at once. Difficult to pin down. It's like nothing I have ever experienced before. I feel so present…

"Yes." I say out loud, which actually startles me a bit. *What had we even been talking about?* I focus my eyes on Josette again and a grin spreads across her face. "Yes, let's do it! Sign me up for 10!"

"Oh wow! Oh… I just knew… I knew when we met on social media…" She trails off, excitement coloring her movements and her facial expression. "So here is what you can expect…" She goes into a lot of detail about the process and what comes next. Apparently, when I said yes, I had signed up for something called "DNA Activation." My excitement climbs to match hers as she continues to describe the process. *I'm in.*

"I'm in!" I exclaim, startling myself again. "I'm in. I can send you the money once I receive a check I'm expecting… I reached out to them last week, so I think the check should be here soon…" I trail off as an image pops into my mind. It's a check I have been expecting from one of my consulting clients. I get a clear image in my mind of the inside of my mailbox, the check sitting in the mailbox expectantly and waiting for me to discover it. *It's here.*

"Actually," I say, "I think… it's here. I think the check is in my mailbox."

I am still feeling completely shocked by the confidence in my voice when she replies, grinning, "Oh, wow! Okay, okay. Go check... do what you need to do. Just keep me in the loop. Make sure you download the voice messaging app so we can stay connected. Drink lots of water, and let me know what comes up for you as we begin this energetic work together. Wow, I have so much to learn from you. I will just... never stop being in awe of all of this. Incredible..." Her voice trails off. I want to stay with her, but she's past the point where I can follow, as much as I yearn to. *There is so much I don't know yet... so much I don't quite understand,* I think to myself. Nothing is quite making sense, and yet, somehow, I feel a deep sense of belonging and understanding that I cannot quite put into words. I feel as though I am arriving... *home.*

"Great! Okay," I say. "Let me see if I'm right about this check – ha! And I'll message you. Wow, thank you so much for this. This feels like magic," I voice a bit breathlessly. *Is this a dream? Why doesn't this feel real?*

Josette smiles warmly. "This *is* magic," she says gently. "It really is. You have no idea."

I breathe calmly, letting her words penetrate my spirit. I know in the depths of my being that she is right.

WAKING UP

I sit up and stretch my arms wide. I have only slept a handful of hours, still buzzing from the beautiful conversation I had with Josette the evening prior.

This feels like magic.

I move my legs to the side of the bed and let them hang for a moment, trying to find the energy to stand up. Surprisingly, the energy flows to me naturally. *That's bizarre... I think to myself. I shouldn't feel so energized. I barely slept...*

Suddenly, I'm jolted out of my own thoughts by a sweet, small voice coming from down the short hallway in our small, single-story home.

"Mama!" I hear my almost 3-year-old son, Finn, say sweetly. It's his way of telling me he is ready to greet the day.

I smile. *Man, I love this little boy.* I quickly use the bathroom, wash my hands, and walk toward his room. The pitch of his voice climbs higher as he hears my footsteps approach his room. I push the door open and see a grin spread across his face.

"Hi, Mama!" he exclaims excitedly.

"Hi, honey!" I crouch down to receive him as he jumps off of his toddler bed and runs toward my open arms.

It is hard to believe that my son is almost 3 years old. My mind wanders to the final days of my pregnancy as memories begin to surface and play quickly in my mind.

"Your baby is breach," the doctor had said to me at my 38-week check-up. She, no doubt seeing my blank expression, felt the need to add some context. "That means he is upside down. He's not in the ideal position for a vaginal birth."

Still feeling confused and shocked, I asked the only question that I could think of, "But... wasn't he just head-down last week?"

The doctor, who happened to be filling in for my regular OBGYN, glanced down at the file in her hands. "Hmm... yes," she said. "It's highly unusual for the baby to turn at this stage of the pregnancy, but he is definitely in the wrong position now. We will check him again next week and see if he's flipped back over."

Panic began to fill my body, and I felt warmth in my face and hands. My pelvis began to ache, and I breathed through it. I had become accustomed to the pelvic pain since I struggled with symphysis pubis dysfunction for most of my pregnancy. Physically, it had been a difficult pregnancy. My movement had been limited due to the SPD, not to mention how triggering pregnancy is anyway for trauma survivors. I swallowed hard and asked the question that was burning inside of me at the moment. The question that I actually knew the answer to but wanted to hear from her, "What... what does it mean if he doesn't flip back around?"

The doctor sighed, appearing to be growing restless. I felt her impatience and annoyance. The curse of being a powerful empath that easily senses the emotions of others. "Then you would have to schedule a C-section with Dr. Jolly," she answered sharply.

"C-section...," I said quietly. I felt emotion rising within me. *I am not supposed to have a C-section... He needs to be birthed vaginally.*

That's the plan. That's the way it's supposed to go. I don't know how to—

"Did you have any other questions at this time?" The doctor's inquiry pulled me out of my anxiety spiral, and I looked up at her, feeling tears forming in my eyes but refusing to let this woman be the first one to experience my vulnerability in this moment.

"No, thank you," I responded quietly. It was almost as though I could feel myself shrinking physically. Further and further away from the present moment. Further and further away from myself.

"Okay. You can schedule your next appointment with the front desk on your way out," she said curtly, her hand already on the doorknob behind her back. She turned quickly and left, the door slowly closing behind her. *Click.*

My toddler son throws his arms around my neck and jolts me back to the present moment.

"Mama! Mama!" he eagerly repeats to get my attention as I stand with him in my arms.

I smile and sigh gently as I say, "Good morning, sweetie!" I look down at him as he lays his head on my shoulder. I breathe deeply, smelling hints of lavender in his coffee-colored brown hair. He is tall for his age and slender, with a little pot belly that sticks out over his pants. He is getting heavier and heavier every day.

He lifts his head from my shoulder and smiles back at me. His light brown eyes are sparkling with joy and his smile spreads widely across his face, "Good morning, Mama!"

As I bring him toward his changing table, I begin to notice the same scorning thoughts that have plagued me for the last several months of this pandemic. *I should have potty-trained him by now…* I think as I begin changing his diaper. I don't necessarily believe I'm being hard on myself at this point. The COVID-19 pandemic started to appear in the US about six months ago, coincidentally, making its first appearance in Seattle. I live in Renton, which is about 10 miles southeast of Seattle, and my husband, Troy, and I have been working from home the entire time.

Sure, juggling working from home and parenting full-time has been difficult, but is that really an excuse to not have him potty-trained by now? I think to myself as I pull a fresh pull-up diaper on him and set him down. As he runs off, I turn around toward his dresser to find some shorts to put him in.

Be easy on yourself, I hear a voice say in my mind.

I stop dead in my tracks and feel warmth in my lower legs, which is my bodily signal that I am receiving a message from the spiritual realm. *Who was that??* I continue to listen, but the voice is gone at this point, as is the warmth in my legs. I shake my head, as though I am shaking water off of my face after a brief swim. *So weird.*

I choose a pair of shorts to put on Finn and absently pull them up over his diaper, as I continue to process what the voice in my head said. *Be easy on yourself. Be easy on yourself.* It's great advice and something I would say to a coaching client.

My thoughts drift off and I allow them to, in service of trying to understand who this voice is and what they are trying to tell me. My mind drifts to May of 2020, just a few months prior when Minneapolis police killed George Floyd, a Black man who was doing nothing wrong. A Black man who was simply living his life as a Black man, which apparently deserved a death sentence. And not just any death sentence… in essence, a public lynching.

His murder sparked national outrage and protests within the US and the world at large. Heated protests erupted in every major US city and many cities across the globe. Cries of solidarity were seen and heard worldwide.

Something happened during that time. Something was released energetically. I felt it when I watched the horrendous video of George Floyd being killed publicly. When I heard him cry out for his mama, I felt it deep within my bones and within my spirit. I sobbed uncontrollably, and my entire body shook with deep, maternal grief. In that moment, he was my child, and I had failed him. I had let him down. Troy saw me and asked what was wrong. I told him, and he went to Finn and asked him to look at me. "Mama is sad…" he had said.

"Sad, mama…" Finn had repeated back.

Something happened in that very moment. The moment George Floyd left the human realm and joined his ranks with the angels, a dam broke. The floodgates burst open, and the violent water was released. Years and years of trauma and pain swept me and so many others up in her flood. I was angry, but not nearly as angry as the Black community. It was as if all of our ancestors, all of our lives from other dimensions, everything had brought us to that very moment in time when George Floyd called out for his mama. I saw several protest signs that read: "All mothers were summoned when George Floyd called out for his mama." That rang so true for me.

But it wasn't just mothers who were summoned. It was all of us. We were being forced to choose a side. I have always believed that humans are inherently good, that we are born into these human bodies as good, divine beings, and that our circumstances and our trauma shape us into who we become. I wholeheartedly believe that we humans are doing the best we can to unlearn the conditioning that has been imprinted on us by caretakers, the media, our neighbors, and so many others. I believe that we always have a choice, and some choose dark paths because they could not find their healing paths. But I hesitate to say that those who choose dark paths are evil; they are simply misguided and misunderstood. They have forgotten who they are on a soul level. They have forgotten their own divinity.

It felt as though, when George Floyd was taken from us, we had entered the next level of spiritual warfare. It didn't feel like a war between good and evil or even right and wrong. It felt like a battle within ourselves, but I had not quite been able to articulate how or why.

All I knew was that a shift had occurred. I had already had a connection with the spiritual realm prior to that tipping point, but my gift became so much more amplified. All of the sudden, I started hearing voices in my head all the time and especially when I was coaching clients in my consulting practice.

It took me some time to understand whose voices I was hearing while coaching. I began to get very curious about the voices, asking in my mind and my spirit who they were. Sometimes they would respond and other times it wasn't for me or even my client to know. One woman who entered my awareness with a message for a client identified herself as my client's mother and was urging her down her divine path. Another client's father came forward with a message of healing and peace. One of my clients had a beloved father figure come forward, the father of one of his best friends as a child, to remind him to play and make time for levity. All of these ancestors and spirit guides who came forward had specific messages for my clients. And all of those messages came back to the same underlying themes: *Trust yourself. Trust your intuition. Be gentle and kind to yourself. Nurture your divine spirit.*

It had been a solid six months that I had been trusting the spiritual realm to provide me with messages for my clients and to help me understand when clients were able and ready to hear the messages they were bringing forward. In the last couple of months, the occurrences began to increase, and I was getting divine messages several times a day.

That increase in frequency was the reason I connected with Josette. I wanted clarity around my gift, and I wanted to understand how to integrate my gift into my coaching practice for the highest outcome, the greatest good. I knew I was put on this Earth to be a messenger, and I had discovered several years back that I had angelic roots; however, what I didn't know was how to best utilize my gifts in the ways that Source had intended for me to use them.

I am lost in reflection and in my own memories when I look up and realize that Finn is smiling up at me. "Milk? Cereal?" he asks and points to the peanut butter cereal above the fridge.

"Oh, honey! Of course. Can you sit in your seat?" I begin to pour cereal and milk into a bowl. He happily stomps off and sits at his small table, and I set the bowl of cereal in front of him. He begins to shovel spoonfuls of cereal into his mouth, slurping loudly as he eats. I pour water into a kettle and begin heating it as I pull a large mug out of the cupboard. I reach into another cupboard and pull out a black tea bag, rip it open absently, and place it in the empty mug. I hear the water boiling in the kettle and turn the heat off. As I pour the water into the mug, I hear another voice.

You're exactly where you are meant to be. You are on your path.

Where is this coming from? Who are you? I ask in my mind. As I close my eyes, waiting for a response, I am startled by a light touch on my shoulder. I turn around to see Troy behind me.

"Sorry, babe. I didn't mean to startle you," he says. "Are you okay?" I look up at him, suddenly feeling taken aback by the concern on his face. His dark brown hair is slightly wet from his shower, and his light brown eyes are looking into mine, seeking. He is a tall guy, a solid foot taller than me, so I have to crane my head to look up at him.

"Oh yeah. I'm just… deep in thought. Good morning," I say and stand on my tiptoes to give him a light kiss on the lips. I suddenly feel a current of energy flow through me. *Whoa… that's weird! What was that about?*

"Morning!" he replies with a boyish grin. I can tell he appreciates the kiss, which is not something I had been giving freely up until this point. Becoming parents has been a tough journey for both of us and has truly tested our love and our patience with one another. Most days, we were just two ships passing in the night, checking in every now and then about what to make for dinner or who was putting Finn down for his nap. And the sex? Virtually non-existent for months at a time. I know it has been tough for him, but I also had not bothered to care. I was too deep in my own resentment to care about his feelings, something that in this present moment makes me feel incredibly sad.

He's such a good partner, I think. *He's such a good dad.*

Suddenly, the current of energy flows through my body again. I focus on it, examining it. I am skilled at noticing, identifying, and putting words to my experiences. This feels like an emotion. This emotion is...

Love, I silently state to myself. *It's love. I'm... in love... with my husband...*

A wave of relief washes over me, gently healing my wounds of resentment. I had been holding on to that resentment since my son was born, silently yet relentlessly blaming Troy for all of the depression and anxiety that had surfaced since becoming a mother. *He wanted this life... he wanted to buy a house, to put down roots... to keep me suffocated in a life I'm not sure I would have chosen for myself...*

I had known it was my despair and childhood trauma rearing its ugly head, even when I was in the darkest depths of postpartum anxiety and grief. Having the awareness did not save me from the tough feelings, and it certainly did not help me rationalize that Troy was *not actually doing anything to me.*

My mind drifts to my earliest memory with Troy, the moment that we met six years prior. I parked my car in downtown Seattle, paid for parking, and looked down at the Maps app on my phone. I was just a few blocks away from the building where a friend from grad school, Anne, was having her birthday party.

I grabbed my long, flowing black skirt and bunched it in my free hand to ensure I didn't inadvertently step on it as I trekked up the steep hill toward the building. I could see the reflection of the pearlescent sequins on my shirt lighting up the space around me.

Once I arrived at the building, I looked up. The skyrise was beautiful, its large windows reflecting the sun which was shining bright on this July day. I pushed a button and was buzzed in quickly. I made my way into the elevator and peeked at my phone again to ensure I knew which apartment I was looking for. I stepped off of the elevator and looked around before heading in what I thought was the right direction.

I approached the apartment and knocked three times. Anne opened the door and her face lit up when she saw me.

"Leilani!" she squealed. "You're here! I'm so glad you came!" I could sense her genuine joy. She seemed a little tipsy, which was no surprise. It was her birthday after all. She looked stunning, her light makeup highlighting her almond shaped eyes and a light pink lip gloss caressed her lips. Her short, light brown hair was gently tussled, no doubt from the shenanigans that had already taken place. I smiled, meeting her joy instantly.

"Happy birthday, friend!" I exclaimed and leaned in and hugged her tightly. Her joy was infectious, and I could sense that she had a great turnout for her birthday. My empath spidey-senses communicated to me that she was feeling a sense of belonging.

After catching up with her for a few moments, I stepped inside and looked around. I knew several people from grad school and waved excitedly. My mind started getting busy, making connections around who I knew and from where while simultaneously sensing the mood of the room. This was normal and a quick calculation I did pretty much every time I entered a new space. It was automatic.

I continued to feel out the room when I noticed a guy in the kitchen, staring down at his phone. He was handsome with dark features, and I instinctively could sense that he was distracted by whomever he was waiting to hear from on his phone. *He has a girlfriend,* I told myself and moved on, continuing to scan the rest of the room.

I spent several minutes making my rounds and catching up with those whom I knew. The energy of the room was electric, deeply joyful and carefree. I was sure it had mostly to do with the sunny weather and the levity of the moment, the celebration.

As the night wore on, the guy in the kitchen introduced himself as Troy, and we found ourselves in easy conversation throughout the night. Laughter was a theme between the two of us. We drank with others, playing flip cup and sharing clove cigarettes. I felt youthful, as though I was in college again. Troy and the others at the party made me feel young again. Carefree. It was a welcome change from the relationship from which I had walked away just weeks earlier. I was tired of feeling so serious, so heavy. I needed to release and experience joy. Troy brought that in droves.

Evening turned to night and eventually morning. We had an instant connection that carried over for several months until he eventually asked me to move in with him the following February. From then, everything moved quickly. We got engaged, got a dog, got married, bought a house, and had a baby. All within the span of about eighteen months. Our love was quick and fiery but so was our conflict. Over time, I began suppressing my needs in order to avoid conflict. It was too intense; we had lost the levity that brought us together that initial midsummer evening when we met. Preserving my peace felt more important than speaking up when things moved much too fast for me. I couldn't keep up, and I felt bogged down by all of the change. All of the expecta-tions. As a fiancé, then a wife, then a mother. I lost myself quickly and fully. Until I was this person. Resentful. Lost. A shell of the person I was when I entered that party so many years prior. And it wasn't anyone's fault but mine. I had suppressed my voice to preserve the peace. I knew better than to blame it on Troy.

In this present moment, as I smile up at him, this love that I feel suddenly for my husband is shocking but also beautiful. It feels like releasing a heavy boulder I had been drudging up a mountain for years. In my mind, I look behind me to see the boulder rolling away, breaking apart with each movement, until it is nothing but specks of sand that are swept away by a gust of wind.

This release. This feels familiar… I think as my mind wanders once again. The wandering from memory to memory, it resembles a dream. In this moment, I feel surprised that the wandering feels so ethereal and not anxiety-inducing at all. It's not overthinking or shuffling through stale memories. It feels… welcoming. Like arriving home. Over and over and over.

This time, I am transported to a meditative session I experienced several weeks ago. I was being led, online, through a guided meditation by a spiritual teacher when I began to sob uncontrollably. At the time, I was grieving the loss of my connection with Source, my higher power. I missed the connection deeply in my body and my spirit, and I began to say out loud, "Why won't you let me see you? I miss you, I miss you, I miss you… Let me see you…"

Suddenly, in my mind's eye, I saw a large, glowing, pearlescent orb of white energy in front of me. It began to get smaller and smaller until it was about the size of a softball. Then it started to move toward me and found its home in the center of my chest.

You see me everyday. I AM you, Source had said to me. In that moment, I felt the anxiety melt away from my body at a cellular level, and my tears dried up. I basked in that peaceful energy for the remainder of the meditation. It was not the first time I had experienced that incredible feeling of Source's presence. There are really no human words to convey how deeply tranquil it is. It's simply a knowing that everything is happening exactly as it is meant to. Feelings like fear, anger, and anxiety are purely human experiences. When we connect with our inherent divinity, those feelings cease to exist for us, and we can experience the only emotions that we, as divine beings, are meant to experience. Feelings like joy and love but also sadness and grief. All of them exist simultaneously. Everything is in balance.

After my meditation ended that evening, I had come out to meet Troy and Finn in the family room. I felt as though I was floating, still on cloud nine from my deeply healing experience. Troy did not seem to notice a difference in me at all, but Finn noticed right away. He hugged me and would not let me go. When it was time for bed, he shrieked when he realized I might leave him, his anxiety growing with each passing moment. Eventually, I decided to bring him into bed with me as he screamed, externalizing his grief. I realized in that moment that he was processing the pain of being so disconnected from me, my true self, my divinity, for the last couple of years. He knew me deeply because we had connected when he was in my womb. He had experienced my divinity firsthand, and that divinity had gotten buried within me once he arrived Earthside. It was replaced by depression and anxiety with the trauma of my own childhood haunting me every day since becoming a mother.

But that was gone now. And he could sense it. And he was processing all of the grief of having lost me the last couple of years.

"I'm here, honey…" I said softly as I stroked his hair. "I'm here… I'm right here… I'm sorry it's been so hard… I'm here…"

Finn continued to wail loudly as Troy entered the room, uneasy. "I'm afraid something is really wrong with him… should we take him to the hospital?"

"No," I said gently, "he just needs to get this out. He's okay, I promise."

As Finn began to calm down and fall asleep in my arms, my thoughts drifted to my own mother. *This feels familiar...* My guides sent me an image of me in my crib, about three months old. I was crying, reaching for my mother who stood on the other side of the room. My cries did not seem to faze her; she was lost in her own thoughts. She stared listlessly out the window, seeming to mentally grasp at something just out of reach. Perhaps the life she would have chosen for herself? I sensed her own feelings of being trapped in her own life, feelings similar to the ones I had held just hours earlier. I sensed her deep depression and anxiety in that very moment before I was transported back to my own bed, holding Finn as he snored quietly in my arms.

I understand now. I understand why I had to experience the depression and anxiety, I thought as I felt synapses firing in my brain. *I had to know these feelings, I had to relate to her experience, in order to find forgiveness for what she could not give me when I was younger. She truly did the best she could. She was not aware that she had choices. She did not know how to be anything other than a victim. She did the best she could. She truly did the best she could.*

Those were my final thoughts as I drifted to sleep, still holding my perfect little boy...

Suddenly, I am jolted back to the present moment. *Whew – all of these memories, wandering through time and space... it's a lot. Beautiful but... a lot to process. What time is it anyway?* I look around for a clock when I hear another voice in my mind.

Time doesn't exist. This time, instead of questioning the voice, I sit with the message.

Time doesn't exist. All of this is happening all at once, I realize suddenly. *I am not getting lost in memories, I am actually moving through time and space. It's all layered on top of itself, and I am experiencing it all at once.*

"Whoa. Fucking wild," I say, out loud this time.

"What was that, babe?" Troy asks.

"Oh. Erm… nothing," I reply. *Would he believe me if I told him?* My gut tells me no. This is my secret to hold for now.

DISCOVERY

As the day wears on, my awareness opens and widens like the aperture of a camera. I try to pay close attention as messages begin pouring in, and I begin to sense that most of the messages are coming from my spirit guides. Every now and then, a spirit comes into my awareness that I sense is not part of my spirit team, but it is usually when I am connecting to someone else's energy, through my coaching or in casual conversation.

The secrets of the Universe begin to make sense, and I feel privy to something very exclusive. *Why me?* I ask myself throughout the day. *Who am I to be able to know these things?*

Although I have been building my leadership coaching and consulting practice for several years, I still work full-time for a well-known, global corporation as an HR program leader. I open my laptop and begin signing into the company network. Once I am online, I look at my calendar as I sip my tea.

Ugh... back-to-back meetings... I sigh, mentally preparing myself for the jam-packed day.

Continuing my corporate role has been a source of inner conflict for me for some time now. I had created the intention to quit my job multiple times, but very earthly concerns always surfaced and foiled my plans. I had convinced myself that I was going to quit three years prior when I was pregnant with my son and fed up with the political bullshit and constant microaggressions.

"Hey, babe," I had told Troy at the time. We were both standing in the kitchen, and I could hardly contain my excitement. "I think I'm going to give myself a birthday present. Please don't freak out, but I'm going to quit my job."

"Wait, what?!" Troy exclaimed, shocked. We had just put an offer on a new home, and I anticipated a bit of surprise on his end, but his reaction, his energy, felt much bigger than I was expecting. "You want to quit now? While we are waiting to close on this house?!"

I stared at him, still feeling a bit stunned at the enormity of his reaction. I felt myself beginning to choose my words carefully, something I had learned to do instinctively over my lifetime; I was conditioned to speak half-truths in the face of big emotions. Anger. Anxiety. It had been unsafe to speak my whole truth for so much of my life, so the shift came so naturally, it was almost painful to notice. "Troy… You know how much this job takes away from me, from my spirit," I took several deep breaths, continuing to search for the words that he might be able to hear. "I… I can't do it anymore. I thought you would understand."

"It's just terrible timing," he continued as he busily opened cupboards to put away the groceries that were sitting in bags on the counter. *He's so mad… he can't even look at me,* I thought to myself. "We are closing on this house, and we have a baby on the way. I just think it's really rash and irresponsible."

The insult in his voice as he spoke the words caught me off guard. "I'm honoring what I want, what I need for myself," I said in a small voice, surprised at how much I sounded like a child as I talked to his… back. He continued to busy himself with his task. "I thought you would understand…" Tears welled up in my eyes. He turned to look at me, his facing seeming a bit softer.

"Look, how about we figure out a plan? Let's move forward with this house, you stay there for a little while longer, and once the baby comes, we can talk about this again… okay?" His hands were on my upper arms now, gentle rubbing up and down as he faced me, no doubt in an attempt to calm me down.

"Sure, okay," I said quietly. These feelings… feeling as though there was no room for my truth, no room for what I needed… they were so familiar. My mind wandered to an image in my mind's eye of myself as a kid sorting laundry. I was the oldest Filipino daughter in a single parent household with four kids. My needs were rarely considered since I was one of the main caretakers for my siblings. My father worked three jobs to keep our family afloat and was always under tremendous pressure, which he externalized often with his quick temper. We lived in poverty by most standards, even though my father was college-educated and military. I rarely voiced my needs, and when I did, they were quickly brushed aside.

My mind gently wandered to the next time I seriously considered quitting my job, which was about a year after the conversation with Troy in the kitchen. It was two weeks before I was due to give birth to my son when I decided I wasn't going back to the same corporate job. I even went so far as to say my goodbyes to close friends I had made at the company over the years.

"I would be shocked if I came back! So, let's stay in touch," I told everyone I trusted with my plan.

However, I quickly found that many of the roles that were available during my maternity leave sounded just as unfulfilling as my current corporate role. The companies who were hiring were not aligned with my values and personified corporate greed. I had some interviews, but nothing really stood out as something

I wanted to do. It was then that I met with my senior manager at the time for lunch, and she basically offered to give me everything I was asking for to stay… a reduced schedule, full flexibility, working from home. She even promoted me two weeks later while I was still on maternity leave. It was enough to put my needs aside once again and settle into motherhood, relying on a familiar work setting as I continued to figure out how to be a mother. My needs were trumped by the needs of others. At least, that was the narrative I told myself.

Be still, my child. This phrase, this voice… it seemed to always come through in my meditations when I considered quitting my corporate job. I got this sense that there was still more for me to do, still impact to be had. *Be still, my child.*

Okay. I'll stay, I often responded a bit begrudgingly.

I snap back to the present moment as an instant message pops up on my computer screen. It's my manager, Zan.

"Hey – got a sec?" the message reads.

"Hi, sure."

He has some questions about a presentation I had prepared earlier in the week. I field his questions easily and prepare for my first call as I sip my tea. It's a coaching call with Mary, one of my mentees.

Oh, phew. Easy start to my day… I tell myself as I begin to call into the meeting.

She and I exchange pleasantries and catch up quickly. Suddenly, I begin to hear messages in my mind, and it becomes very clear that one of her spirit guides has a message for her.

"Mary, this may sound a little hard to believe…," I start. "But… I may have a message for you, if you are willing to hear it."

"Oh, sure!" she replies.

"Mmm… I am not sure you understand," I clarify. "I… hear spirits. I have an open line of communication with the spiritual realm, and someone has come forward to talk to you. Are you open to hearing this message?"

The line becomes silent for several seconds as she, no doubt, considers what I have just said. This isn't the first time I have had to have this awkward exchange with people while in my corporate role. Spirit guides have been coming forward more often over the last several months, but today is different. The line of communication is wide open, and there is no question in my mind who is coming forward. It's her mother.

"Yes," Mary says quietly, almost inaudibly. "Yes, please tell me."

"Okay. It's your mother. She's passed on, right?" I start. I cannot see Mary's face, but I can practically hear her jaw dropping.

"Yes," she replies, and I can hear her voice crack with emotion.

Please let her know… how proud of her I am…

"She says she's really proud of you and the ways you are taking care of your family, including her brother, your uncle," I say, and pause. I have learned over the last few months that people need some time to process the information I convey to them. After a few moments, I continue. "She says you have been taking better care of yourself lately… thinking through your boundaries. Does that resonate?"

"Yes, it does…" Mary is still in shock, but I continue.

Her boundaries…

"Have you been having trouble setting these boundaries with your family?" I ask gently.

"Yes, I have been feeling so guilty about it," she responds. "If I don't take care of them, who will?"

I consider the question and send it up to Mary's mother and the rest of her guides.

It's time they learn…

"Your mom says it's time they learn to do these things on their own. You have done enough, you always have. It's time to live your life independent of them. You didn't sign up for this, and you can let go of the burden of taking care of them. It's been long enough."

Mary is in tears, sobbing quietly at this point. I give her a few moments before starting again.

"Is there anything you want to ask her?" I inquire gently.

"My mom?" Mary asks, seeming stunned. "I can do that?"

"Yes, of course." I smile. People are often taken aback by the fact that the communication moves both ways.

Mary seems to consider the question for a moment. "Is she happy? Is she at peace?"

I know the answer, but I send it up out of respect. It is a common thing that humans ask of their deceased loved ones, and the answer is always the same.

Yes…

"Yes, she's happy and very much at peace," I reply. "She said it was instantaneous. Once she passed on, her suffering ended, and she was one with the divine realm. It's quiet and peaceful there. And she wants me to remind you that she's always with you. You've been sad lately about the fact that she won't see you get married and have children?"

Mary begins to sob again, more heavily this time. "Yes… it's really been on my mind lately…"

"She's with you. She always will be. She also tries to communicate with you. Please make sure you're spending time alone, quieting your mind. She says you hear her sometimes. Trust that it is her coming through." I breathe deeply, allowing the information to permeate.

"Okay," Mary sighs, seeming to internalize the guidance. "Okay, I will. Thank you so much, Leilani… you have no idea what this means to me…" I smile and gently cut her off.

"I am only a channel, like a telephone line," I say. "No thanks needed. Take good care of yourself, Mary." I hang up with her and sigh. I stand up and walk into the kitchen. I pick up a bundle of dried sage, the bowl of salt next to it, and a lighter and walk outside. Troy and I have had a lot of discussions about how uncomfortable he is with my burning sage in the house. My mind drifts to the most recent argument we had about it.

"I wouldn't light up a cigarette in the middle of the house…," he had said pointedly, as if it were completely ridiculous that I would even consider it.

"It's not the same," I had rebutted, defensively.

Over time, and after some relationship coaching, I had finally gotten to a point where I didn't even mind going outside to burn it, as long as he didn't judge me for having to do so.

Burning sage, or smudging, is a ritual I have adopted over the last few months, as the frequency of divine messages that I was receiving increased. It was something that a spiritual healer had told me would help with releasing the energy of the people I was coaching and the spirits with whom I was interacting.

In this moment, I walk outside into the backyard and light the small sage bundle. As it begins to smoke, I slowly move the sage all over my body, focusing on my throat chakra and my heart chakra. Usually, I can feel an energetic shift when I do this; however, this time, I feel very little. *That's odd.*

I bring everything back inside, grab a glass of water, and sit down at my desk. I think ahead to my next meeting, which I anticipate will require a little more energy on my end – a coaching session with an executive named Dan. The company where I work is extremely hierarchical, so those of us who are not in management generally have to be cautious about how transparent we want to be. I have heard the cautionary tale of the career-limiting candor that colleagues of mine have navigated firsthand, so I have always been guarded around how much to share and with whom. This particular executive is a fairly safe person for me; however, I still feel as though I have to put my façade on. This is an automatic thing at this point. It's called code-switching and I learned it early on in my conditioning while growing up in Oklahoma. I turn on the charm, turn down the "angry woman of color" persona, and diplomatically sidestep career-ending landmines as I navigate the *just right* amount of candor where I can be seen as a truth-teller… yet, still have a job.

However, this time feels different. As I click on the meeting notice link, I imagine the façade that I typically wear, its exterior weathered and battered, representing the wounds it has endured time and time again after being in corporate America for 13 years. And in the last several months, my mask has begun to crack and crumble at the edges as I have experimented with speaking a bit more truth with each encounter, energetically pulling on the collective courage that people of color, and especially the Black community, have been externalizing since the racial unrest began.

As the online meeting room begins to pop up, I imagine the façade again and notice something strange. Pieces of it are beginning to fall away… slowly at first, like grains of sand in an hourglass, and then increasingly faster, like desert sand being swept away by a windstorm. The ferocity of the image catches me off guard as Dan's video pops up on the screen. He seems distracted and doesn't notice when I enter the virtual meeting room, his eyes moving quickly as if reading something on his computer screen.

"Hi Dan! How are you?" I say, noting his lack of attention while simultaneously trying to make sense of the mask that, at this point, is completely gone.

"Hey, Leilani…" he says, continuing to appear distracted. "I am just processing something, an email I received from one of the employees in my organization." He goes on to describe the email. This employee had expressed her disappointment about the lack of communication from him specifically about the murder of

Black people by the police. She was also critical of the communication that had been sent by our CEO, stating that it was too safe and vague. "Her email really motivated me to send a communication to my employees, and I was hoping to get some feedback on the content."

We spend some time reviewing his message, and I find myself being extremely candid with my guidance and feedback. *Whew – where is this courage coming from?* I ask myself, careful not to examine it too closely for fear that it could leave at any moment. After speaking with Dan for a few more minutes, he thanks me for my coaching and honesty, and we hang up.

I sit back in my computer chair for a moment, still feeling stunned by my lack of diplomacy on the call. It isn't like me to give such unfiltered feedback, but it came naturally and without fear. *It felt good…* I thought to myself. I take an extra moment to soak in the pride that I feel for myself before transitioning to the rest of my workday.

***

As I shut down my computer for the day, I find myself quickly processing the events that occurred. *I… didn't give a shit…* I say silently, which I realize right away isn't completely true. *I mean… I cared but not about how I was being perceived… not enough to censor myself. Huh…*

What feels even more miraculous than my lack of self-censorship was the reception I received from others when speaking my truth. *They appreciated it… they welcomed… even… craved it…* I bask in feeling as though I was on fire all day, regardless of who was on the other end receiving the message. I had a meeting with a vice president and displayed the same amount of candor. I was, of course, mindful that my message was conveyed with care, but the message was crisp... clean... informative... helpful. Honest.

In this moment, I imagine myself as a clear channel for the divine realm. *I'm just interpreting,* I think to myself. *I'm... interpreting the exact message that their spirit guides are trying to get to them... I'm simply a conduit.* I breathe deeply into that awareness, feeling suddenly purposeful now that my mask has been dissolved and carried away. Speaking my truth is part of my purpose... because, often times, "my" truth is actually the truth coming from the divine realm.

Whew – that's intense. It's a big job... I think as I gently seek guidance from my spirit team.

Yes, I hear them reply. *It is. And you are so capable of the task.*

I smile, soaking in their affirmation as I breathe deeply. Then, they are gone.

LAVENDER

It is early evening, and somehow it feels as though a lifetime has passed and no time at all since I spoke to Josette just the evening prior.

Time doesn't exist.

That phrase… it makes so much sense now as I process the images that have been sent to me all day from the spiritual realm. Time is a construct. It is one of many constructs that we, as humans, have created to try to convince ourselves that we have any semblance of control, that some type of order exists. Time doesn't exist, at least not in the linear way that we have been conditioned to believe our entire lives.

An image appears in my mind, no doubt sent from my spirit guides helping me make sense of my experience. They show me an image of a timeline my father had created of my childhood. It's several pieces of paper taped together, with tick marks for different points in my childhood. Birth… 2 months old… 3 months old… 6 months old… each tick mark has a small description and a photo…

A photo of me as an infant, peering out from under a light blanket, my chubby arms attempting to push myself up, and a giant smile on my face. *Lani at 2 months old. Honolulu, Hawaii.*

A photo of me as a baby, sitting in a high chair, and looking at the camera while the rest of my face is buried in a large piece of watermelon. *Lani at 6 months old. Honolulu, Hawaii. She had stolen her brother's watermelon and began to eat it when we were not paying attention.*

A photo of me as a small girl, in a jean jacket, jean skirt, and tights. My hair was heavily teased and pulled up in typical 80s fashion. *Lani at 5 years old, 5th birthday. Balibago, Philippines.*

The timeline that my father had created stopped at my 5th birthday, but my guides add papers to the mental image in my mind. The papers are taped together as my father had done, and my guides add photos of various points throughout my life, up until the present moment. To my surprise, the papers continue, and they add visuals of memories yet to be lived or experienced. Rather than still photos, these memories are moving images, short videos playing inside my mind's eye. My son's first day of college… dancing with him on his wedding day. Troy and I slow dancing in a beach house at night, dimly lit, as waves crash on the beach. Me on my death bed with my son gently holding my hand, whispering, "You did good, Mom… you can let go…"

Suddenly, the long, paper timeline of my life begins to move as a whole, and it begins to fold over onto itself, creating gentle flowing layers of time. A bright, thin light begins to move into the folded papers, starting with the top and penetrating each layer. Slowly, the bright light expands to encompass the entire timeline.

A voice enters my awareness, and it feels different than my guides. Bigger. More authoritative.

It's Source. The message is crystal clear. I am being informed of one of the many universal truths that will flow my way over the next several days.

Everything exists in this present moment. The past, the present, and the future. They all exist here. And you have access to all of them. All at once.

I am shown an image of my keys sitting on my desk in my office. They are not in their typical spot hanging up on the hook in the kitchen. Suddenly, I am reminded of my uncanny ability to find things I have misplaced. Typically, all I have to do is retrace my steps and I can see the scene replay in my mind with accurate detail.

Am I remembering? I ask. *Or... am I...*

You are accessing the fluidity of time, Source responds, finishing my thought. *You are going back to that moment in time, briefly, to 'remember.'*

So, does memory even exist? Or are we always just moving through time?

I sense Source smile. *Memory exists.* Nothing more is said, and I get the sense that it is all I get to know at this point.

I suddenly feel a bit small, unworthy. *Why me?* I ask. *Why am I allowed to know these things and others are not?*

Because this is part of your mission, Source continues. *This is your highest calling. And there are things that you will know and others cannot know. Not just yet. That is the way your gift manifests. You are an etheric translator. You can hear me, you can hear the spiritual realm. You are the one who will know what to say to others and when to bring them along. You are the one who will reach many with your message.*

Your message, I say in correction with a playful smile.

Yes, okay. I can almost hear the amusement in Source's voice. *My message.*

Okay... okay. Show me the way. I am your messenger. Thank you for choosing me.

Thank you for saying yes.

And then they are gone.

***

The words "highest calling" continue to resonate in my mind, over and over again, hours after my conversation with Source. I have always sensed that we, as humans, are put on this Earth to fulfill some sort of calling, some sort of work, which is divinely inspired and guided. However, the confirmation, which came straight from Source, has me buzzing in this moment.

I am outside, walking our big, burly golden retriever, Sampson, as this notion of our highest calling continues to swirl around in my mind. I stop walking as the lavender bushes in my neighbor's front yard capture my attention.

The bushes are so fragrant that my body instinctively moves toward them; my senses are overtaken by the beauty of their perfume. I am filled with a calm clarity as I begin to pay closer attention. Something that I have realized over the last several days is when my guides, Source, or some unseen power is getting my attention (in this case, via my sense of smell), I stop and become present. I pay attention. I listen and watch for the inevitable message on its way to me.

I notice bees. Lots and lots of bees, undoubtedly drawn in by the fragrance of the flowering lavender plants. *Why have I never noticed all of these bees?* I ask myself. I must have walked by these lavender bushes a dozen times in the last week, and I have never seen this multitude of bees. I lean in closer to observe them.

They are working busily. They seem to be doing their own individual work, but somehow it's all connected. Some stop at the same lavender buds before moving on to a different bud. I notice a few bump into each other, but they do not seem to mind or notice. *It's expected. It's expected to bump into one another. It's expected to cross paths. And there is enough for everyone. There is enough.*

I stand up suddenly.

There is enough. There is enough for everyone.

The warmth in my lower legs confirms there is something important here, something worth noting. Something worth filing away.

We humans… we have gotten it wrong. Again. We are so busy being in competition with one another, striving to prove ourselves, to lock down resources, that we are missing it. We are missing something very big…

"Our highest calling," I say out loud. My lower legs get warmer as I continue to process.

My mind drifts to a recent memory, a conversation I had with a consulting client recently.

"I understand if you are unable or unwilling to do this… I know it is a big ask…," she says. She is the executive director of one of my biggest clients, a local non-profit. She has asked me to facilitate a conversation with her board of directors about women of color leaving the board. I am immediately uncomfortable with the ask, and the voice of one of my dear friends and business partner, Adana, enters my awareness. I can see her in my mind's eye: her beautiful brown skin and brown eyes framed with retro glasses, curly blonde hair falling softly around her face.

That's a heavy fucking lift. That's what Adana would have said to me. I shake off the thought as I imagine myself putting on my "good girl" mask. My good girl mask is something I am used to wearing at this point. As a 37-year-old woman of color, I have become very comfortable in my good girl mask. It's my people-pleasing mask, the one that strives for unattainable perfection. The one that conforms to White culture, inside and outside of work. The one that masks my depression, anxiety, and deep imposter syndrome. The one that desires so desperately to fit in. It's the one that says "yes" to heavy fucking lifts, regardless of the personal toll it takes on my well-being.

"Yes," I hear myself say. "Yes, I can do that."

"Oh, gosh! Fantastic," my client says back to me. "I just feel so much comfortable knowing we will be in your capable hands. I know the others will be thrilled as well."

We exchange goodbyes and hang up the phone. Several minutes later, my phone beeps. It's an email from my client. She is thanking me for saying yes and giving me one last out, stating that she would completely understand if I was not comfortable facilitating the discussion.

I respond quickly, seemingly before I lose my nerve. I let her know I feel comfortable with the request and capable of leading the conversation. I thank her for checking in one last time.

I had so many opportunities to say no, I say to myself in this present moment, observing the bees working amongst the lavender plants. *My intuition was screaming at me, telling me: "What the fuck are you doing?!" And, instead of saying no, I can actually see myself putting on my good girl mask and saying yes, as my insides crumble into a pile of anxiety and dread.*

I continue to draw upon the memory, observing myself anxiously prepping for it and entering the video call several days later. I see my own face on the screen, surprising even myself with my calm and composed exterior. Inside, every single intuitive alarm is ringing so loudly that I can barely make out the words of those speaking on the call.

I move through the motions, facilitate the discussion as I promised I would, and they never see me sweat. It isn't until I hang up the phone that I burst into tears, holding the center of my chest, almost as an unspoken apology to my broken spirit.

Afraid of waking my son, who is sleeping in the room next to my office, I grab my phone and stumble into our family room on the other side of the house. I fall onto the couch, still clutching my chest and gripping my phone tightly with the other hand. I am gasping for breath, trying to reason in my mind.

Why? Why? WHY?! Why did I say yes?! I scold myself. *I knew. I knew from the moment she first asked. I knew. Why did I say yes?*

As I continue to process what had just happened on the call, I don't believe that anything too far out of the ordinary happened. In fact, if any of the attendees on the call knew about my sudden and significant emotional reaction after the call, I know they would be stunned. I kept my composure. I was the good girl.

But inside… Inside I was so deeply in my despair from trying to facilitate this discussion that was so triggering and that I was so personally intertwined with that, now that I was able to remove my good girl mask, my spirit came crashing down, hard. This is the "yes" that broke me. The "yes" that followed my intuitive knowing that the answer was really, "Fuck no." It was the first time I had actively ignored my intuition in my business and chosen people-pleasing instead.

The constructs. The constructs are what led me to that "yes." The constructs that say I needed to be a good girl. That I needed to fit in. That I needed to please my clients at any expense. The constructs that say that there is not enough to go around, especially not for women of color. The constructs that say I don't get to say "no" if I want to "make it." If I want people to like me and if I want clients to refer me.

In this present moment, as I continue to stare at the bees buzzing around the lavender buds, it begins to make more sense. The constructs. They need to come down. They are keeping us in competition, keeping us separate. Pitting us all against one another, but when we are quiet and truly listen, we can hear so clearly from the divine realm: *There is enough. We are enough.*

We have been divinely ordained to do *something* here… to complete our highest calling. And if we truly stand in our power, if we begin to trust that inner knowing which tells us what that highest calling is, there will always be enough. We will have enough creativity. We will have enough resources. We will have enough work. Source will never let us down, never let us fall, if we let go of our attachment to these man-made constructs and begin to trust our truth... trust universal truths.

I better get to work, I think as I move past the lavender bushes toward my house.

***

I am sitting at my desk, staring at a blank page in my journal as my mind buzzes with possibilities. It's as though reflecting on that good girl memory has opened the flood gates of my highest calling, and I am getting a personal download from Source about what my work looks like.

Coaching. Executive coaching. I write it down as it begins to flow toward me. *I am leading a group of leadership coaches and consultants.* Names of coaching colleagues begin to flow to me, and I begin creating a business structure. I am labeling each part of my business.

Coaches. Consultants. Admin/accounting. Marketing. Youth retreats. Women of color retreats...

The information is flowing to me so quickly that I have difficulty capturing it all. Some of the names and their roles do not surprise me while some surprise me immensely.

Huh, I think to myself inquisitively, *I'm not sure I would have ever thought about that person for that...*

But I trust it. I trust all of it, and I capture all of it. Once the information is done flowing through me, I sit back in my chair and take a look at what I have written down, what I have co-created with the divine realm. I have the sense that this is a first draft, that this business structure will likely change a bit, but it is a starting point.

It gives me some clear direction.

Yes, I say silently to myself. *This is something I can say yes to.*

KY ARRIVES

It is evening, and I think back on the day. I can hardly believe that it's only been a little more than 24 hours since I talked to Josette.

It is 10:30 PM, and Troy and Finn are both sound asleep. The late evening is my favorite time of day when I can easily find stillness. It is when I can be creative and imaginative without interruption. In addition to Troy and Finn being asleep, much of the world is asleep as well, which matters because I am a powerful empath. I take on the feelings of those I do not even know and have never met simply by existing in this human realm. And when people are sleeping, I can finally find a small amount of peace in my spirit.

I breathe slowly, allowing the gentle sounds of meditative music to enter my aura through my earbuds. I breathe a few more times, gently reflecting on my day while also mindfully integrating the wisdom I have acquired throughout my day.

My thoughts are interrupted by a text I receive on my phone. I look down to see who it is. Ky.

An image of her enters my mind's eye. Big, brown eyes, always seeking and perhaps never finding. Olive skin. Long hair that flows well past her shoulders, which seems to be dyed a different color every time I see her. Her looks are striking, and she turns heads everywhere she goes.

Ky is my oldest niece, my sister's daughter. She has had a tough life. She has an absent addict father; my sister does the best she can to give her what she needs, but she is only one person. I have always had a soft spot in my heart for Ky. She is so sweet and intuitive; she has always been reaching, seeking. For love. Validation. Meaning. She has always tried so hard to make sense of life and, many times, has come up short. She has attempted suicide several times in her short eighteen years on Earth. I tend to drop everything I am doing to respond to any distress signal I receive from her.

I read the text she sent me again: "I just can't do it, Auntie Lani. It's feeling so hard. Everything is so hard... what do I do?"

I immediately call her, feeling the despair in her text. I sense intuitively that I am being activated and mobilized to support her. I feel warmth in my lower legs. Something important is happening in this moment.

"Hello...," she says almost inaudibly when she picks up the phone. I immediately sense her sadness, which is not uncommon when I talk to her. But this time, it's different. Heavier. I had asked her to call me if she ever feels suicidal again, and I knew this was one such time. I take a deep breath and imagine my protective bubble, ensuring that I don't internalize her pain. It would make her feel better if I were to take it on, to internalize it myself, but it would be debilitating to me. I know because it's happened to me several times with her and so many others.

"Hey, Ky... what's wrong? What's going on?" I ask gently, reaching out to her energetically to understand her emotional state.

After a few moments, I hear her begin to quietly sob as I feel my heart breaking. *I hate this...* I think to myself. I always feel so helpless when she feels like this. I continue to reach out to her

41

energetically, this time in a sort of emotional embrace. As I do so, I hear her breathing begin to slow.

"I just…," she says, her voice low, "I just don't know how much longer I can do it… It's all feeling so hard and usually you are the one I would talk to… but ever since we started working together, it feels as though I can't talk to you. At least… not the way we talked before…"

I think back to about a month ago when I asked Ky to help me with my business. I needed some administrative support, and she seemed interested in learning more about what I do.

"Do you want to run my social media for me?" I had asked her.

"Sure!" she said, seeming to be genuinely excited. "I mean, I'm already on social media all day… at least this way I can get paid for it!"

I brought her on because I genuinely disliked that part of the business—it always felt so forced. And I still struggled with being completely authentic on social media. I would just rather some-one else handle it.

Over the span of a couple of weeks, each time Ky and I talked, it was about the business. She would text me a few ideas for posts, and I would choose one and send her a write-up for a caption. Our relationship went from having deep, meaningful conversations to daily business tasks. She was the first to acknowledge the differ-ence in the way we interacted, and, although I noticed it, I honest-ly had not thought too much about it.

Now, in the present moment, with her clearly feeling alone and unseen, I begin to see the full impact of our drifting apart. I had always assumed it was a temporary rift, like something we would figure out as we continued to work together. But the reality is very different. She is suffering, and, in this moment, she does not have me as her trusted confidante. She has no one.

"You just feel… far away…," she says between sobs.

Suddenly, a powerful urge sweeps over me. *She has to keep going,* Source tells me. *She has to keep speaking her truth…* I nod and shift my focus to her.

"Say more. How are you feeling right now? What do you need to tell me? It's okay, Ky. I can handle it, I promise." My voice becomes lower, more welcoming. It feels important to do everything I can to get her to speak through the pain, through the fear.

"I can't…," she sobs. "It's too hard." I feel my anxiety begin to creep up as I picture her slipping away from me toward what seems to be a dark void behind her. I don't know what is in this void nor do I want to find out. I continue to engage her.

"You have to," I assure her gently. "You have to speak your truth, despite the shaking. Despite the fear…" I feel as though I am begging at this point, my voice now barely above a whisper. I imagine sending her energy, urging her to continue, to find the strength to move toward my voice.

"I just… you…," she says quietly, as if telling a deeply held secret. "You are… my person… and lately, I'm not saying it's your fault… but…," she pauses, seeming to consider her words carefully. I can sense her mind racing, trying desperately to find the perfect words for this moment, the words that won't hurt me.

"Please," I urge her. "You have to say this. Just say it. It's okay." I begin breathing deeply and imagine blanketing her with a soft glowing pink light. *Please give her the strength to speak this truth,* I beg Source.

"I just feel really let down," she says, almost as though she is rushing through the words before losing her nerve. "I just… you're my person. You're the only one. You're the only one who sees me, who gets me… and ever since… ever since we started working together, our relationship is all about work. It's all we ever talk about. I miss you and the ways you used to support me…" She is now sobbing uncontrollably, and I feel a rush of energy charge through my body. I close my eyes and ask the ether how to proceed.

Stay with her… keep her here, now…

"Is there anything else? What do you want in this moment? Right here and right now?" I ask gently, lovingly. I continue to send her energy, hoping that she will sense the genuine care in my voice. And although I am trying to send her love, I feel as though I'm on the edge of the void with her. I am reaching for her while trying to desperately grab at the Earth… trying to find something firm, something solid, to prevent us both from falling to our demise into the void. It's dangerous and precarious yet also necessary and… somehow divine. It's all of it all at once.

"I just… want things to be back to normal," she says quietly, almost breathlessly. Her breathing begins to slow and in my mind's eye, I see her tears begin to slow and eventually dry up. "Holy shit. That was really hard."

"Yeah, I know," I respond, relief washing over my entire body. My anxiety begins to dissipate and in my mind's eye, I see it falling toward the bottoms of my feet, through the hardwood floor, past the foundation of our home, and into the Earth to be nurtured, recycled. "It's hard to speak your truth to the people who really see you. But know that I love you, and I do see you… I really, really do…"

We sit on the phone together for a moment, and I glance down at my watch. 11:11. I begin to realize that the energy of our conversation has shifted. Something is very different.

Did I just…? I begin to ask silently.

Yes… I hear a voice respond. *Yes, she's here on this side with you now.*

O…kay… What exactly does this mean?

You will see.

***

The next couple of hours fly by as Ky and I unpack what just happened. I tell her about Josette and how my spiritual gifts have been completely open the last 24 hours. I tell her how spot-on I have been about everything and how I have been an open channel to the divine realm. I tell her that I have been privy to secrets of the Universe that no one else is allowed to know just yet.

"Whaaaaaat?! This is so wild...," she said. After I had realized what had happened, I saw an image of how I had actually pulled her into the spiritual realm with me.

The image in my mind's eye was so vivid, it was as if I was actually there. Ky was sitting cross-legged next to a dark, bottomless hole, rocking and holding herself in a tight hug. She was teetering nervously on the edge of it, tears streaming down her face. I could sense her emotions, her energy. She was ready to give up, to let go, and allow herself to fall into the darkness.

As I described the image to her, she saw it in her mind's eye as well, as if I had pushed the image to her telepathically.

"I would have died," she said. "If you would have let me fall, I would have left this human realm."

I took several moments to consider what she had just said. "You're right. That would have been it. That would have been the end." A tinge of pain and sadness washes over my body as the words leave my lips. Tears begin to form in my eyes, and I blink them away. *She's here. She's still here. And I did that.*

"Yeah...," she continued. "It wasn't the first time I had been on the edge. I am thinking of all of my other suicide attempts. And I don't think it's the first time you pulled my ass out of that hole either. Like, 'Oh, hell no... no, you don't, bish! Not today!'"

We both laughed loudly, a welcome release. She's so right. As she described it, I saw it in my mind's eye as well. She was about halfway to falling completely into the void when I reached into the human realm, grabbed her almost violently by the shirt, and dragged her across the threshold to this side, the spiritual realm. And her heightened awareness and ascended consciousness happened almost instantaneously. We spent the following two hours practicing our gifts together. Ky is incredibly clairvoyant, or "clear seeing," meaning that she can communicate with others through images in her mind's eye and can even see visions before they have come to pass. She is also clairaudient, or "clear hearing," meaning she receives and sends messages as sounds in her mind. We were practicing communicating to each other in our mind's eye, pushing images to one another through the ether. As we continued to explore the possibilities, we started to realize that these clair-abilities of ours are also how we commune with the spiritual realm. The realm that is basically layered on top of our human realm and only truly "seen" by those of us who have been brought to the other side.

We also talked about the term *starseed*. "Do you know what that is?" she had asked me.

"Actually… not really…" I replied, thinking back to the evening prior when Josette had used it casually in conversation.

"I think…," Ky had said, "I think that I… am a starseed." She went on to say that she thought she came from another planet, that she had always felt that way. My jaw hit the floor as I considered that possibility.

"Whoa! Oh my gosh…," I said as confirmation began flooding in from the spiritual realm. "You're right! Whoa!" My head began to feel light as information continued to make its way to my consciousness. The information I was receiving was completely from Source and the spiritual realm, but nothing in my own body felt like I knew anything about this possibility. I just sat in awe as I listened to Ky speak her truth and noticed every time Source affirmed her thoughts.

There is so much I still don't know! I replied, continuing to feel awe-struck.

Now, as we both blink through exhaustion, we finally say our goodbyes. I glance down at the time again. 2:22 AM.

"I love you, Starseed. Drink lots of water. Get some rest."

I sense her smile on the other side of the phone. "I love you, too, Auntie Lani. Good night."

FINN ARRIVES

The next day flies by as a blur. I have never felt so present, so much in every, single moment. It is intoxicating, and I continue to lean into it.

I quickly realize, however, that it is easy for me to get lost in that feeling; the feeling of being so high up in the ether that I forget to take care of the earthly things. Things like my human body. Tasks around the house (I quickly find that these are the most useless and inefficient use of my time and energy). I think I'm taking care of my son well enough… I'm feeling joyful and childlike. Nothing that used to trigger me even gets close to drawing a reaction from me, like his constantly reaching for me and pulling at me. It used to draw a trauma response, and I would feel myself having a visceral reaction to his constant touch and my lack of autonomous, physical space. But now… now, I can't get enough of him and his touch. I want to eat him up.

Ah, so this is what motherhood is supposed to feel like. Who knew?

I also notice I am quite scattered throughout the day. I start tasks around the house, like doing the dishes, only to get distracted with a funny video on social media. Then, I remember the dishes, and a short time later find myself drawing with crayons with my son. There is so much information in this present moment, and it's so easy to be distracted.

Oh man... Now I know how Troy feels much of the time!

I think back to the times I have been hard on Troy for starting a task and abandoning it halfway through, blaming his lack of ability to concentrate or stay focused. I cringe as I think about the ways I would react... rolling my eyes, harsh judgment, contempt. Now, as I am on this side, where being 100% present is so easy for me, I am experiencing a type of poetic justice.

Troy comes into the kitchen and sighs.

"Babe...," he says, sounding exasperated. I look up from the drawing I'm co-creating with Finn. "I thought you were going to do the dishes?" He points at the half-empty, open dishwasher.

"Oh yeah! Thanks for reminding me...," I stand up from my son's tiny art table and make my way to the sink. Troy watches me, seeming to make sure I actually start the dishes again before walking toward the refrigerator to begin cooking dinner.

I can tell he notices a difference in my behaviors and demeanor, but I cannot be sure to what extent he truly sees it. I feel as though I am physically unable to hold back my truth and the truth of my current, spiritual form. I feel so far away from my typical, ego-centered self, and, if I am truly honest with myself, I am in love with the feeling of it. The ego, the human consciousness, is often so heavy and bogged down. It convinces us that our experience is singular, solitary. The higher consciousness, our spiritual body, is truly formless. We are energetically connected to every single person, every plant, animal, and element on Earth. I cannot make a single move without it impacting many, many things down the line, like a row of dominoes that splits off into multiple rows and continues to do so into infinity. The possibility of that, the butterfly effect of our actions, is something I hold with enormity and simply see as truth. It is a spiritual truth that I am so connected with in this very moment that nothing else seems to matter... like, doing the dishes.

I sigh audibly as I see Troy out of the corner of my eye, no doubt watching to see if I actually stick to the task. *I better get to it...*

***

It is 7:17 in the evening, and Finn is now splashing around in the bathtub. While I'm bathing him, I hear Troy rustling around in Finn's bedroom, putting a sippy cup of water and a snack cup with crackers on his bookshelf. I hear Troy stomp off toward the kitchen and begin to hear the sound of pots and pans banging around as he cleans up our dishes from dinner.

I pull Finn out of the bath, water mixed with bubbles dripping off of his toes as I wrap the towel around his little body. He's surprisingly accepting of the exit from the bath this evening, which is not a normal occurrence. He typically expresses discontent whenever I even suggest that bath time is ending. He loves being in the water that much.

I can't blame him, I think, reflecting on the last few days and how I have prioritized Epsom salt baths in my bedtime routine. I am reminded of how healing it feels to be in water lately... a departure from the fear I felt in water only weeks prior. Now, I stay in the water as long as I possibly can.

I bring Finn into his room and pull on a diaper and a cozy set of pajamas with planets and stars printed on them. *Seems fitting,* I say to myself, but I am not entirely sure why. My mind drifts to Ky for a moment, and the word *starseed* enters my awareness. As Finn searches for a book for us to read together, I stay with the thought for a moment.

Starseed... I allow the word to sink into my consciousness as the thoughts continue to form. *Is... Finn...?*

"Mama! This one!" Finn says, jolting me out of my daze. He's grinning from ear-to-ear and holding his favorite book with a cartoon T-rex on the front.

"Okay, buddy! Come on up!" He climbs onto my lap as I open the book to the first page and start reading it aloud. We read a few books before it's time for lights out. I reach over to his bookshelf and turn on his sound machine, allowing the soft sound of crashing waves to gently waft around the room, before I click off his white owl lamp.

He is still cozied up to me and sitting on my lap. He knows the drill as our bedtime ritual has been the same since he was six months old. We rock in his cozy green rocking recliner as we say our daily gratitude and prayers, then we sing a couple of songs together. It is always the same.

This evening, however, something is a little different. As we begin the second iteration of "Twinkle, Twinkle, Little Star," I notice other music. For a moment, I am confused, wondering where on Earth the music is coming from. I lean my head toward his window, straining to hear any noises outside.

Nope, that isn't it… What in the world…?

Then it dawns on me. *It's coming from his sound machine.* I lean in closer and hear crisp, gentle notes flowing over the sound of the crashing waves. It sounds like a synthesizer, and the tune is dreamy, as though it could be a lullaby. *Whoa – so bizarre…*

After a few minutes of listening to the ethereal, modern sounding music, it gently fades out and we are left listening to the sounds of the crashing waves. I am still rocking with Finn when he begins to hum two notes. Somehow, I immediately recognize the notes as C and G. The C is drawn out for a couple of beats and then the G is one beat. *Weird that I would know the notes…*

"Mmmm-mm… Mmmm-mm…," Finn hums quietly. I intuitively begin humming along with him. "Mmmm-mm… Mmmm-mm…,"

I am still rocking with him in the recliner as we hum the tune over and over. Our humming gets louder and louder and I feel energy pulsating between us. I don't even think to question it. It feels right in the moment.

He's… he's guiding us… I think to myself. *Okay, honey… I'm here. I'm here with you. Where are we going?* I say in my mind, willing him to receive the message.

"Mmmm-mm… mmmm-mm…," We continue to hum. Our humming continues to escalate in volume, louder and louder. I have a fleeting thought that Troy can hear us. Is he confused? It doesn't matter.

"Mmmm-mm… mmmm-mm… mmmm-mm…," Finn's humming begins to get quieter and quieter, and I match his volume as the humming fades out. "Mmmm-mm… mmmm-mm… mmmm-mm…"

Finn stops humming, but I am still rocking him. I take note of the energy that is still moving between us. The energy that, at the height of the humming was supercharged and vibrant, has now dulled to a gentle current. Finn takes my hand in his, and I feel a small jolt of energy as I continue to rock with him, his head resting gently on my chest. I kiss the top of his head.

Out of the corner of my eye, I notice faint lights on the ceiling. I crane my head back and focus my eyes upward, unsure that I have actually seen anything. Suddenly, I begin to see more lights, sparkling and dancing across the ceiling. They look like brain synapses firing; neural pathways gently lighting up. It begins to make sense to me, and I get the feeling that Finn is communicating with me telepathically, helping me understand.

My brain… It's… expanding… opening up. I get a quick download of information, remembering that the brain is still a mystery to our species. *When our consciousness elevates, our brains evolve… we use our brains… differently… more fully…*

"Coooooooool..." I hear myself say out loud, as I continue to watch the lights dance across the ceiling. After what seems like an hour, but was likely only about a minute, the lights begin to fade, and I instinctively begin slowing the rocking until the chair is still. I stroke his hair as I sit in awe for a moment at my beautiful, talented boy. And then it hits me...

"Honey!" I whisper. "Did I just bring you over to this side? Or... I guess I should say... did you just bring yourself over?!" He tele-pathically sends me confirmation. He's here. I hug him tightly, and his little arms hug me back. He wriggles off of my lap and walks over to his bed and lies down. I stand up and gently pull his blan-ket up to cover his body. I can tell he is already drifting off to sleep.

"Sleep well, honey. I'm so proud of you. Good night." I gently kiss his forehead before I leave the room. I stand just outside of his room for a moment before I head straight into my bedroom and fall into a deep sleep.

THE VEIL

The next day, I wake to the sound of Finn's voice echoing through the hall.

"Up… down! Up… down!" He is singing the two words, over and over, in the same tones as the humming from the night before.

I glanced down at my watch, which is still on my wrist from the night before. 7:42. I sit up and stretch my arms wide before standing up. I make my way down the hall, still hearing his voice.

"Up… down! Up… down!" I slowly open his door and his attention shifts to me right away. "Mama!"

"Hi, honey!" I say, brightly. I am eyeing him at this point, extremely curious about what is to come. *What happens now? Am I supposed to be bringing people over? Is that my purpose? Is he supposed to help me? What's next?* I do my best to calm my racing thoughts as he runs toward me, embracing me in a sweet hug. I melt into it and wrap my arms around him. "Hi, sweetie…"

"Water? Water?" he asks, and I reach for his sippy cup, which is still in the exact same spot from the night before. I hand it to him, and he begins gulping it down quickly.

As the morning wears on, I find myself staring at him at various times, deeply inquisitive. I don't know exactly what I'm looking for, but I'm enthralled. *He seems so normal…* I think. But I do begin to notice that I'm much quicker to pick up on what he wants. It's something I've always been fairly good at; however, this takes it to a whole new level. All he has to do is think about something, and I instinctively know what he wants.

And he continues to sing the tune, "Up… down! Up… down!"

"What does that mean, buddy? What is up, down?" I ask, but he just smiles back at me and continues to sing.

***

Later in the day, I find myself lying in bed, the plush down comforter pulled up to my chin, and suddenly, I feel like a little girl again. Bright sunlight is streaming in through the large sliding glass door of our master bedroom. It is early afternoon, and I am almost giddy with excitement as I savor the first moment I have had all day to reflect on everything that has happened since the night before. Now that Finn is down for his nap, I breathe deeply and begin to process the information I have received from the spiritual realm over the last few days. Josette had mentioned to make sure that I was recording my thoughts, whether I send her voice messages or not, so I pick up my phone and begin recording my voice without having any intention to send the message.

I am currently processing this notion of balance and re-balancing. The word that I have been using to talk about the separateness between our human existence (what we are seeing, hearing, and feeling with our five senses) and our spiritual existence (what exists beyond the constructs of our human, ordinary reality) is the veil. I have seen this veil in my mind's eye, and it generally looks the same each time I encounter it. It looks like a mirror, stretching for miles and miles, but when I get closer to it, I realize it's water. It is a thin, glassy sheet of water, suspended in the air. It's similar to a waterfall, but it's not moving as a waterfall does. It just *is*. Unmoving. Unwavering. Seemingly untouched.

As I interact with the veil, I notice I can move freely between the two worlds. On the human side, I can see for miles up and down the veil in either direction. I feel shocked by how many humans are right there, either right up against the veil, or already beginning to move through it.

"Ascension is happening, with or without me," I say out loud. I notice how much of an ego-centered thought it sounds like through the lens of my human consciousness. But when I say it through my spiritual consciousness, I know it's not based in ego. I'm simply trying to understand.

"What is my purpose here, if people can make it through the veil without me?" I ask out loud. Silence.

I begin to think of my own journey crossing the veil. The last three years, I have been so deeply embedded in my human consciousness, lost in my depression and anxiety. Deep grief and sadness. Consuming outrage and resentment. I imagine a grandfather clock and the pendulum that swings from side to side. In the middle of the downswing, where the pendulum is at its lowest point, I see a small veil take form.

On the right side of the pendulum is my human self. All of the ways I've been lost in my consciousness, in this human construct, for three years. I was so far over into the human realm that I, as the pendulum, was violently banging against the wood of the clock, over and over again. The right side of the clock was beginning to weaken, the wood wearing down with each violent encounter of the pendulum… each encounter of *me*. The wood was cracking and beginning to create sawdust. Three years is a long time to be in my human suffering.

2020 has been a year of slowing down. The violence of my up-swing began to slow several months ago, when I began interpreting messages from the divine realm, as though the wonder and awe I felt of the spiritual realm was distracting me from my own suffering. I had stopped banging against the side of the clock and slowly began to make my way toward the veil, toward the center of my downswing. Sure, every now and then I would still move toward the right side of the clock, toward my human suffering, but I didn't stay there long anymore. I would touch briefly and find myself moving toward the center of my downswing again. I had found balance. Re-balance.

Then, I met Josette and said *yes* to ascension. At the time I said *yes*, my spirit was all-in, but my humanness had no idea what I was agreeing to. It didn't matter. Ascension still occurred, with or without my human comprehension.

That is when the swing to the other side occurred. But not just to the other side of the veil; the pendulum moved clear over to the other side. It wasn't violent like in the ways it interacted with my human, ego-centered side. Instead, it floated lightly to the spiritual side, the divine realm, and continued to move gently just next to the edge of the clock. It stayed there for a while… days? Who knows? Time doesn't exist.

But in this moment, lying in my bed with the covers pulled up to my chin, giddy with realization and feeling privy to se-crets others are not able to know yet, I observe this clock, this divine metaphor manifesting in my mind's eye. I see the pen-dulum begin to float downward, toward the center, and even-tually toward the veil. I expect to see it land right in the center, and I am surprised when I see it moving gently left, right, left, right… interacting with the veil every so often, but moving so seamlessly between both worlds that the movement is almost unseen. Subtle. Gentle. Slight.

"Is this where I am supposed to be? Right up at the veil, barely moving between it?" I startle myself with the sound of my own voice, remembering that I have been speaking out loud this entire time, processing this current thought, this metaphor.

I listen intently for a moment before I hear the voice in my mind.

Yes. You are exactly where you are meant to be, Source replies.

"But I want to stay here, floating gently, fully in the ethereal realm. I want to be here with you. It's so much more peaceful here, so much quieter, much more loving."

I understand, child. And… you chose this.

"I chose this? What do you mean?"

You chose this task. You chose to be a transition guide. You chose to assist others with their ascension. You love them all so much, you chose to be further away from the perfection of the divine realm in order to bring others along.

I consider that for a moment. "Well… okay. Yeah. That sounds like me," I say into my phone, giggling a bit at my predictability.

Suddenly, an image enters my mind's eye. A man, someone so familiar that I recognize him instantly. Jesus. Literally, Jesus.

"Oh. Erm. Hellooo…," I say, unsure of exactly how to begin communing with him. Prior to this exact moment, I had questioned whether Jesus was real. I grew up with the notion of Jesus as humanity's savior as something that was pounded into my head and, subsequently, my heart. I learned very early on that questioning the existence of Jesus as humanity's savior was completely forbidden, not only at church but also at home. Questioning was completely off limits and quickly squelched.

In my adulthood, I had let go of that expectation and began to question his existence. I had settled on the notion that Jesus was probably a prophet, someone important… but the Son of God? Dying for our sins? Nah. Probably not.

However, in this moment, he is here with me. I'm still unsure of all of the narratives, who he truly is—to us as humans, to the divine realm. All I know is: Jesus is here, with me.

The image of Jesus in my mind's eye is vivid. He looks slightly different now than I remember him looking in paintings and images I had seen growing up. He's tall and... not exactly slender... but lean, like a laborer. I can tell he has a little muscle hiding under his clothing. He is wearing a cream-colored shirt and pants, and the material is flowy but still a bit stiff... linen, maybe? And he doesn't have light shooting out of his head or anything, like I remember seeing in the images. He looks... normal. Like a regular guy. Handsome. Kind of hot, actually.

"Hello...," I say again. "You... are Jesus."

Yes, he replies with a slight grin.

"Um... you know... you're *kind of* a celebrity here. You know that, right?" I ask, feeling a bit playful now.

Um... YES. Yes, I know that, he replies, seeming to play into my exchange.

"And...," I begin again. "You're... pretty fucking hot!"

This time, instead of replying, he laughs loudly, grabbing at his belly, as if he cannot contain his own amusement. *You're ridiculous!*

I laugh. "But seriously! Why does no one talk about that?! How did I not know how hot you are?"

He is still grinning when he replies: *Humans see what they want to see.*

My laughter calms until all that is left is a giant smile on my face. "That's deep, Jesus." And then, Jesus... *actually* rolls his eyes at me, amused. "But wow, really. I get it. Thank you."

He takes a long breath before continuing. *I have some things to tell you. You are special. You have to know that, embrace that. You have some work to do here. But you are not doing it alone. You have the entire divine realm with you. All of the angels, all of the ancestors, all of the guides. And not just yours… truly ALL of them. We are all here with you. It will be beautiful and brilliant and you are so, so worthy. We need you to step into your power, to trust it. To trust us. To trust Source.*

I feel tears beginning to form in my eyes, feeling the truth of his words, the impact. Several moments pass before I form a response that feels even the slightest bit worthy of what I just received. "Thank you, Jesus. Thank you for the message… for trusting me with this… this work. Whatever it is. Thank you. I just hope I don't let any of you down."

You won't, he replies. *There is no possible way you could. We're just so glad you said yes. Keep leaning into it all. Keep being present. Keep being curious. Keep saying yes.*

And then he is gone.

I blink for a few moments and realize I am still recording my voice. I hit stop and take a deep breath. Suddenly, out of nowhere, I think of my grandmother. I have been on this side of the veil, entwined with the ethereal realm, long enough to know what that means: I need to call her. There is something waiting for me, a lesson, on the other side of that call.

I am still under the covers when I pick up my phone to find her number in my contacts and hit dial. Her answering machine picks up. It is the standard robotic voice asking to leave a message, then I hear a beep.

"Hi, Grandmama! It's Lani. I just wanted to see how you were—" My thought is interrupted by a *click* and the sound of my grandmother's voice.

"Hi, Lani? Are you there? It's Grandmama," she says. I instinctively connect with her energy and feel her simultaneous feelings of surprise and joy to hear from me.

"Oh! Hi, Grandmama! How are you?" I say, truly grateful to hear her voice on the other end. This was the first time we had talked in far too long… years, perhaps? My siblings and I had had a falling out with her and much of that side of our family since my little brother, Lawrence, died about 16 years ago. He was almost two years old when it happened. He had drowned in my grandparents' swimming pool in a horrible accident. I was much older because my mom had Lawrence in her second marriage much later in life. I had lived with them for about six months while I was in college and had grown very close with Lawrence. When he passed away, I was devastated.

My mind drifts to that time so long ago, my little brother's wake. My youngest sister, Kris, was holding a photo, sobbing, and placing the photo gently into the casket where my beautiful little brother's body lay, still and peaceful. My sister had waited until everyone in the room had spent time with his body before walking up slowly, sobbing, with her boyfriend at the time, Steven, by her side.

"Nooooo!!!" I heard my grandmother's voice pierce the silence from the other side of the room. "No, you don't have the right! You don't get to grieve him! This is your fault! This is your fault!" She was screaming, and I could see in her eyes how deeply lost and angry she was. Instinctually, I leapt out of my seat and ran to my sister's side as I saw Kris and Steven registering the shock of the outburst.

"She has a right to grieve!" Steven shouted back, holding my sister as she sobbed.

"What the fuck did you say?!" My uncle, Derrick, had screamed at him. He rushed him, posturing. Ready to fight. He lifted his fist and I instinctively got between them. I hugged Steven with my entire body, doing all that I could to block my large body building uncle from having any access to him. I felt my consciousness separating from my body, something I was used to doing when bracing myself to experience trauma. I barely felt the heavy punches that I was absorbing with my back while blocking Derrick from landing blows on this 16-year-old child who was simply protecting his girlfriend.

My mind snaps back to the present moment. My grandmother and I had been exchanging surface-level pleasantries for several minutes. We had been talking about my family, my son, my job. She had talked about COVID and how terrified she was of contracting it, "This will kill me, La'ni... if I get it, that's it for me..." In this present moment, I take a deep breath, intentionally holding space for her fears before I notice my guides gently urging me to have the conversation that I am meant to have with her in this moment.

"Grandmama," I begin. "I... have this urge to tell you something, but I'm not sure how you will react..." I wait to hear her response before continuing.

She seems taken aback for a moment, seemingly surprised by the vulnerability in my voice. "It's okay, Lani. You can tell me. I'm listening," she urges me gently.

"Okay," I breathe, mustering up the courage to say what I know I am meant to say. *How do I even say this?* I ask my guides. Silence. "I... am very connected to the spiritual realm..."

"Oh?" she says, pausing briefly and seeming to digest the information I just shared with her. "What do you mean, sweetie? Connected how?"

"Well...," I say, continuing to plead with my guides to find the words. Silence. *These words have to be mine. I have to have courage. Just say it...* "I have always sensed spirits and now, I have a really strong connection to them. Like, I hear them. They talk to me all the time. They are talking to me now." I give her a moment to let my words register. To my surprise, she doesn't skip a beat in her response.

"Oh. Oh, yes, that is not surprising to me," she replies, seeming to draw from her memory. "I have always known you were special."

I am completely taken aback by her nonchalant reaction. "What do you mean, Grandmama?"

"Just that, Lani. I have always known you were special, ever since you were a little girl," she continues. I feel tears forming in my eyes, feeling the weight of her words. I did not expect her to be so accepting of my gifts, and I certainly did not expect her to affirm how *special* I was… how special I am. "But, Lani… you have to be careful with that. It's really easy to invite evil that way. But yeah, my mother had that gift, too."

The line goes silent for a moment as I consider what she just said. "So… this isn't surprising to you?"

"Oh, honey, no. Not at all. It seems like this type of gift… it runs in our family. I didn't know you had the gift but, like I said, I've always known you were special. It doesn't surprise me that you have it. And I never liked how they treated you."

I consider her words, trying to grasp what she means. "What do you mean by that, Grandmama? You didn't like how *who* treated me?"

"Oh, you know. Your mama," she says. "And your dad. They would always say things like, 'Oh, Lani… *mula-Lani*… they would treat you like you were stupid. I always knew differently. I said it when you were just a little girl. You were always so sweet, and I knew you were smart and gifted. I told them: 'You watch. She's special. She's different. Don't treat her like that. She's not *mulalà*.'"

I feel hot tears forming in my eyes as I am transported back to my childhood. I am surrounded by my siblings and my parents. Everyone is much, much younger. I look down at my hands, my body. Little hands. I look at my brother. He's about seven or so, which would make me about five years old. They are all laughing and looking at me.

"*Mula-Lani!*" They are saying, pointing and grabbing their sides. Laughing. Laughing at my expense. *Mulalà* is a Filipino term which translates to stupidity or ignorance. In this moment, as a little girl, I feel hurt but also a part of something. I feel a bit honored to have a nickname, but I also don't quite understand the meaning of it. As time begins to fast-forward, I realize I have internalized this nickname my entire life. My family always treated me as though I was a bit absent-minded, aloof. A little oblivious. Gullible. Innocent. Naïve.

Now, in this moment, lying in my bed as an adult, and with my grandmother on the line affirming me, I begin to sob. I am healing and releasing in this moment, releasing the pain of growing up around people who thought that, just because I was different, just because I was and am a pure soul, that I was not smart. That I was naïve. Less than. That I didn't fit in.

"You didn't deserve that," my grandmother continued. "And now, look at you! Look at who you've become! You are so special. So gifted. So successful. You have a beautiful family. You have a good job. You have a good life. You have done so well, Lani, and I am so proud of you." I can feel her joy coming through the line, and I feel the tears fall from my eyes and roll down my cheeks.

"Thank you, Grandmama," I say as I grab a tissue from the bedstand and wipe my eyes and nose. Suddenly, I notice my grandfather appear in my mind's eye. Her husband. I smile. "And... Granddaddy is here."

"He's here?" she says, and I can hear her trying to comprehend.

"Yeah, he's here with Lawrence." I see them both so clearly in my mind's eye. My grandfather looks as he did when I knew him toward the end of his life. Pale, white skin with a wrinkled face and a mischievous twinkle in his bright blue eyes. His face was weathered and also held so much love and joy, lots of smile lines. Short and soft gray and white hair. Lawrence looks as I remembered him, a couple of feet tall and holding my grandfather's left hand. Pale, soft skin and piercing blue eyes. Chubby cheeks and a toothy grin.

I can hear her smile on the other side of the phone as she undoubtedly considers the image of them both appearing. "Lawrence is here with me a lot, I think."

"Yes," I reply. "He is. Granddaddy, too. They just want you to know they see you. They look after you."

"Oh, yes. I know," she says. "I can feel them, especially Lawrence. Sometimes, I can feel him hugging me… at night, in my bed." Her voice cracks a bit, and I feel the emotion in her admission.

In my mind's eye, I see my little brother, still holding my grandfather's hand, nod excitedly. "Yes, he does that. He is saying he does that a lot."

"I know…," she says, her voice continuing to crack as emotion pours forward.

"Grandmama, I just need you to know that this conversation and what you just said… that you have always seen me as special," I start, channeling the words now because my emotions have completely gotten in the way, "…it means something. I have felt stupid a lot of my life and I never quite knew why. I always had good grades. I was always helping everyone. I couldn't understand it. What you gave me today… it's a gift. It really is. Thank you for always seeing me as special and treating me like I was. Thank you for telling me all of this now. It's so important. You have no idea…" My voice trails off as emotion takes the words out of my mouth. I breathe in deeply and exhale.

"Of course, Lani. You are special," she says. "I just… I want you to be careful. Be careful because there are bad spirits out there. You have to make sure you're being safe. That you're protecting yourself. You don't want to let someone in that could hurt you."

I feel a bit jarred by her repeated warning but collected myself before responding. "Yes, I hear you. Thank you, Grandmama. I love you."

"I love you, too, honey. Call me again soon, okay?"

"Okay, Grandmama. I will. Bye." I click the button to end the call and set my phone on the bedstand before turning onto my left side and falling into a deep sleep.

NIRVANA

It is midday the following day, and I am laser-focused on a task for my corporate role when my concentration is interrupted by my phone ringing. I peek at it to see my dad video calling me from the Philippines. I hit accept.

"Hey!" I greet him, smiling.

"Hi baby," says my dad, peering down his nose through his bifocals. I chuckle to myself as I consider how much he is looking like an old man these days.

"Hi Dad! I'm just working. What's up?" My dad and I are close, and I welcome his calls when they happen, which isn't often. My relationship with my father has evolved over the years, and I'm grateful that we are at a place where I look forward to connecting with him.

"Just checking to see how everyone is doing."

"Everyone is fine, as far as I know," I reply. I know exactly what he's asking. Ever since my dad retired to the Philippines about three years ago with my stepmother (Nanay, as we call her), I've become, by default, my siblings' honorary parent here in Washington. It's the role that I have taken on in my family for much of my life.

"How about Jac?" my dad asks. "Is everything okay with her? I am worried about her money situation. I know she can't work during COVID."

Prior to retirement, my dad was in the Army for 34 years as a nurse, medic, and eventually, a hospital administrator. He had worked his way up the ranks from an enlisted soldier to an officer and eventually to the rank of lieutenant colonel. He is easily one of the most hardworking people I know, and I'm grateful that he modeled a solid work ethic for me.

My dad moved to Hawaii from the Philippines with my mom and older brother back in 1983, shortly before I was born. When I asked him recently why he moved to the States, he said he wanted to create a better life for his family and better than what he experienced growing up in Balibago, in the Philippines. About nine months after I was born, he became overwhelmed with the cost of health insurance for a family of four and joined the military.

Some of my earliest memories are seeing my parents grinding and trying to create a better life for us. Although my mom, a mixed Filipino and Caucasian woman, grew up in the US, her parents were not wealthy, and her family of origin was also a military family. My grandfather was a proud Navy man who grew up poor in the American South during the Great Depression. Both of my parents had shame wrapped up in money and working. Fortunately, my dad acquired a bit of wealth for himself as an officer in the Army and has been able to release a lot of that early shame. But, like any good father, he still worries about our livelihoods.

"I think she's okay. She hasn't indicated to me otherwise," I reply.

"Well...," my dad says, contemplating my response. "Can you just make sure to check on her? Let me know if she needs anything please."

I sigh. "Sure, Dad."

"How about you? How's Pin-Pin?" That's the nickname that he and Nanay have for Finn. It's a very Filipino thing to do to nickname children repeating one syllable of their name. Kris's daughter Natalie is "Nat-Nat" and Jac's daughter, Stella, is "Tell-Tell."

"He's doing pretty well, other than being cooped up at home with us all the time while we're working... poor guy," Just then, I notice my dad's parent's, my grandparents, coming forward to speak with my dad. "Actually, Dad... I have something I want to tell you."

"What's that?" he says, his attention wavering to something on the TV screen in front of him.

"I... have been communicating with the spiritual realm lately. Like, a lot," I say and study his face, looking for a hint of his reaction.

"What do you mean?" he says, his attention now on me again but his facial expression unchanged.

"Well, practically ever since COVID started, I've been communicating with spirits. Or, I guess, they mostly communicate with me. It's usually relatives of someone I'm talking to or some kind of guide or angel. Right now...," I pause and take a breath, "Apu and Tatang are here. They want to tell you something."

I can see my dad considering this thought, his expression contemplative. He turns to get my stepmother's attention. "Nel! *Mekeni!*" he says, and they exchange a few more words in Kapangpangan, our family's native language, before my stepmother walks over and sits down next to him. "What are they saying?" my dad asks.

"Well, they're just really proud of you... both of you," I start, closing my eyes so that I can focus in on the message that is so clearly coming through. "They are saying you've both been through a lot, that you're survivors. You've come a long way." Suddenly, an image appears and I begin to describe it. "I'm not sure what this means, but they are saying you will know, Dad. I see water… and you and Nanay are holding hands and standing, facing them. Nanay is in front of Apu, and Tatang is in front of you, Dad. Apu and Tatang are holding hands and have golden light behind them, silhouetting them. It's getting brighter and brighter. What does that mean, Dad?" I open my eyes and study my father's face. His eyebrows are furrowed and his forehead wrinkled as he considers the information.

"Well," my dad says, still seeming to carefully consider the message. "That is the Philippines. The sun always comes out behind Mt. Arayat, our mountain here. It is my east marker. And as for the water…" He looks contemplative for a moment. "Well, there's always water. Water has always been important to our family, dating back several generations. We were farmers, and it helped us maintain the crops, our food and that of our community. Now, the water is more harmful, causing floods, damage, and other destruction. Apu and Tatang grew up in Macabebe, which is flooded and has been for years now. I wonder if that's what they're showing us…" His voice trails off, and he seems to be seeking his own intuition to put the pieces together. "I think they are telling me to stay in the Philippines, that I have work to do here. I think they're saying that I can help our people."

In my mind's eye, I see my grandmother smile and nod. "Yes," I respond. "Apu is saying yes." I smile, silently thanking my grandparents for sending him the information he needed in the moment.

"Okay, we will stay," my dad says definitively, the contemplation now nowhere to be seen in his face. "I have been worried about you all there in the States, but I think I have more work to do here. I have more *good* to do here."

"I think you're right, Dad. And I know you will do so much. Our people need you." I look over at Nanay, who is crying now. "Nanay, they want you to know that you are gifted. You see the signs and the ways they are trying to communicate with you both. You will see the signs and communicate them to my dad. You're the interpreter, and he's the doer." I smile as I digest that simple truth, one that I have observed since Nanay entered our family so many years ago. "They are saying to trust yourself and the messages that come through. Your role is important: you will be showing my dad what needs to happen. You're both important to our community there."

"Okay," Nanay says, very matter-of-fact, as if accepting the mission. "I see things and I hear them… I just tell your Dad?"

"Yes, that's all you have to do. And you're really important in all of this. Dad can't move forward without you. You're important to each other. You need each other," I interpret the final message coming through. "You need to continue to cherish each other. They're proud of you for everything you have been through together. But you need to really focus on treating each other well."

My dad hugs Nanay and kisses her forehead. "Yes, I know," he says.

"I love you both. Thank you for listening and accepting me," I add, feeling genuinely grateful for their openness.

"We love you, Lani," my dad replies, and I can see him choking back tears. I have only witnessed my father cry three times in my whole life, so his tender emotion catches me a bit off guard. "Bye, baby." And then they are gone.

I put down the phone and inhale deeply. My mind drifts to earlier days, back when I was a child, probably about 3 or 4 years old. My dad would argue with my mom about information that she was receiving via her intuition. I don't remember specifics of any argument, but I know this: he didn't believe her. He questioned her ability to commune with the spiritual realm, to transcend space and time, to exercise her divine gifts. I always got the sense that he thought she was mentally unstable, even though he never pointedly expressed that.

In this moment, I begin to make connections about how my beliefs around my spiritual gifts (and what it even means to have spiritual gifts) have been molded by his disbelief of my mom and her incredible abilities. I have always held a bit of conflict around psychic abilities. I have vivid memories of hurting myself when I was in grade school. I would bump or bruise myself inevitably and go to my mom for comfort.

"Come here, honey," my mom would say and I would sit next to her. She would hover her hands over the injured area and breathe deeply. I could actually feel the pain dissipate, and my mom would hold the energy between her hands before raising her arms above her head, sending the energy into the ether. The pain would change from being sharp and shooting to feeling like a dull ache; I would instantly feel much better.

I would contrast those types of experiences with the sentiment that I would feel from my dad, and over time, I began to question my mom's ability to actually take pain away. I would watch her, judgmentally, and after she would send the energy up to the ether, I would walk away feeling slightly annoyed and internalizing the narrative that she was just a little detached from reality.

This created a lack of acceptance within myself for my own spiritual gifts. When I look back on those memories now, I can almost see myself putting away my gifts. *I had to tuck them away in order to feel loved,* I think as tears form in my eyes. *When you bring your spiritual gifts forward, people see you as mentally unstable and won't want to be with you. It created fear of not belonging because of my gifts.* I check in with my guides to see if I'm on the right track. I sense nodding.

And now, I continue, *my dad accepts me and all of my gifts. He didn't even question them.* I think back to another memory about seven years ago. I was in my early thirties and co-facilitating an overnight retreat. I was lying in bed, about to fall asleep, when my breathing slowed considerably. My body began to feel light and I could actually feel my consciousness rise up out of my physical body. I felt as though I was floating just above my body when I was suddenly transported to a vision.

I knew it wasn't a dream because of how I entered. I was lucid, and then suddenly, I was somewhere else. The vision was vivid and so real, which is not uncommon for my dreams, but there was this intuitive *knowing* that this was something more. Something important.

In the vision, I am on a bus. I look around, and I am the only passenger there. When I peer up at the driver, all I see is a flood of golden and white light. I cannot see the driver but I know instinctively that I trust them and that they are taking me to my future. They are guiding the way, and I have no control over the journey.

I look down at my palms and notice two images. In my left palm, I see the blurred image of a man with dark hair and a strong build. In my right palm, I see a young boy. His hair is chestnut brown, and he is grinning broadly, missing a front tooth. He is about 5 or 6 years old.

My husband and my son… I say to myself, instinctively knowing exactly who these people are. *This driver is taking me to them. And I don't have to do anything.*

The realization is a relief, and I feel my body relax. I breathe deeply and look out the window for the first time. We are on a bridge and all I see is water that spans miles and eventually blends with the horizon. The sun, which is shining brightly amidst a clear pale blue sky, glistens against the water, making it seem as though diamonds cover it completely. Stars, perhaps? The entire scene is a dance of light, water, magic, and Universal energy. I watch in awe for several moments before I am transported back to my physical body.

I continue to breathe deeply before acclimating back to the present moment, the retreat space. I feel a deep sense of peace and knowing… perhaps residual from the vision I just saw. I notice one of my co-facilitators enter the room, and I sense her emotions. She is anxious about another facilitator with whom she has been in conflict all weekend. I have no way of knowing that except that I feel her emotion, her worry. It feels surreal to experience it as if it were my emotion; however, I know it does not belong to me. I am simply an observer. I am separate from her experience, and I have a profound perspective on it.

Without thinking, I pick up my phone and begin drafting an email to capture the thoughts that are moving through me with fierce momentum.

Ultimate awareness. Seeing glimpses into my future and being in awe. Seeing a husband and a son. No specifics. No anxiety. No need for fear. Feeling outside of my body. No explanation and no fear. Just now, in the physical realm, Sam enters the room and I'm seeing her conflict. Seeing her pain. Seeing her worry aimed toward Chasity. Immediate and surreal awareness. Seeing her fully and not being afraid for her. Trying to convince her that there is no struggle here. There is no fear or anxiety. I'm ok feeling her pain. My heart rate increasing. I have awareness of it. It is not beating out of my chest. It is not painful or piercing as it often feels. It is not panic. I am seeing all of the pain; I am sensing it all in this moment. The pain of my friends and family. Of the world. So much pain.

Seeing my friend Randy's pain. Heartache. His years of hurt. His pain and struggle to overcome and be the best man he can be. For his family. For his wife. For every single person he has even met or truly seen. He fights for them. Mostly he is fighting for himself. He is fighting for his hurt self. I see him as a young boy. Scared and alone. Ill equipped to take a stand. Scared. Terrified. Alone. He is so alone. So alone. I want to hold him. I want to hug him. Not because I fear for him. There is no fear. There is no anxiety. I have felt the calm. I see Source's capable hands. Holding us all. Guiding us. They are smiling at us. There is so much pain, but they smile because there is no reason to be anxious. We are their children and part of their plan. I have seen a glimpse of their plan. I'm so unworthy. But I have seen it. It is this feeling of calm. A life beyond this. A life without pain. There is no fear or anxiety because this new life, with all of its purity and beauty, is a certainty.

I see my sister. I see her struggle. I see the world. Full of pain. Lacking connection. Everyone wanting it so bad and trying so hard and unable. Unable to connect. But there is no anxiety. There is no fear. Because their capable hands engulf us all. Source connects us and binds us together and we are seen by them if no one else. Every day. All the time. I see the sorrow and I weep. Not because I am sad, but because Source is so capable. I weep for the world. They will also see. Someday. That there is no need for fear. Because the pain will pass. Perhaps not in this life. But their hands surround us. They are capable and strong. They have a plan. A sense of calm that engulfs me. It controls my body. I am outside of myself. Ultimate awareness. There is no judgment. Source is not judging me or you, my human siblings. They accept me. I am a vehicle for them. Their message. This message. I'm not worthy. I am relieved. In this moment, I am healed.

There is a deep well of pain in this world. Grudges. Lost connections. Pride. Things standing in our way. Not allowing us to just trust each other. Love each other. Forgive each other. Forgive ourselves. Connection in its purest form. Nirvana.

I see the hurt in each of us. People in my life. People I have met. People I pass on the street. People I have never seen. Our pain. Our anguish. Our struggle. I see it all yet I do not weep for it. I weep because we are all okay. We are struggling so hard, but we are all okay. There is no fear. Source is here all the time. There is no burden because they carry it for me. Love in its purest form.

I'm ready. Ready to share this message. There is no anxiety around it. No embarrassment. No fear of judgment from others. Only joy. Pure joy. I am a messenger; it is so clear. I have to share this message with so many others. My heart is calm thinking that some may not receive it. That's okay. We are all okay. Beliefs. Faith. It is all irrelevant here. Sharing the message is most important. There will be cynics. There will be judgments surrounding me, yet my heart refuses to race. I am a child of Source. I think of my friends and my family, all of the people with whom I am meant to share this message. And there is so much pain. I'm overwhelmed by it but not sad. Because there is no fear. And Source's hands are capable and strong. They hold me. They hold all of us. My human siblings. It is so quiet and peaceful here.

I send the email and set my phone down before falling into a deep, dreamless sleep.

Later that week, I had called my dad to describe the vision to him and the message. I winced after telling him, bracing myself for his inevitable reaction, the disbelief with which I was sure he would respond. Instead, I was met with a long silence.

After what seemed like an eternity, he cleared his voice and began speaking, "Lani… I have been a devout Catholic my entire life, and I have never had an experience like what you just described." I felt the pang of sadness, of longing, in his voice.

"Yeah, Dad," I replied, after waiting a moment to see if he had more to say. "It was pretty unreal."

"That was the Holy Spirit," he added, helping me understand his thought process. "You were touched by God. What a gift."

"Yeah… it was beautiful," I said, feeling taken aback by his vulnerability, his willing acceptance of my admission. "I'm not sure why I was chosen, but I was. I think I'm supposed to share this message with as many people as I can."

I heard nothing but silence on the line as he, no doubt, formulated his next thought. "I'm proud of you, baby."

"Thanks, Dad," I reply instinctively, tears forming in my eyes. Those were not words that I heard from my dad often. Not because he didn't feel that way but because he is a man of so few words.

Hearing them in that moment felt foreign, like seeing an animal completely out of place, out of its element. But I allowed warmth to cover my body from head to toe as I felt myself internalizing his words. We ended the conversation soon afterward, and I plopped down onto the couch of my small Seattle studio apartment.

In this present moment, I think back to the shock that I felt so many years ago surrounding his acceptance of my gifts, my message from the ether. "My dad has healed," I say out loud, and I see my guides nodding, confirming my current thought. "He has healed his brokenness around spiritual gifts, his interpretation of spiritual gifts as a sign of mental instability. He is believing what is already true: that we all have these gifts, and we must lean into them in order to move humanity forward to the next evolution of our human collective."

And you did that, they add. *He trusts you, and you helped him heal. Now he will have a much bigger impact because he is willing to trust the unseen. He's willing to consider the possibility that he can't know everything nor can he fully know the mystery of how Source operates. He is willing to question his own belief system. He is arriving home to himself and remembering his divinity. All because you said yes to stepping into your wholeness and sharing your truth.*

I breathe deeply, allowing the truth of their words to permeate my cells. "I did that. I said yes. And…," I consider my next thought. "I must continue to say yes in order to fulfill my mission here."

It's always a choice, they add. *You always have free will. But yes. In order to have your highest impact here, in this realm, in this dimension, saying yes is required.*

"Saying yes is required," I repeat, internalizing the mantra. "How do I know when to say yes and when to say no?"

You're a clear channel, they reply. *You will know.*

And then they are gone.

LIMITATIONS

It is finally the weekend, and we are piled into Troy's truck. Finn is in the back watching a TV show on his tablet with Sampson next to him, panting as he sticks his head out the window, allowing his large ears to flop around in the wind.

I look over at Troy and smile. He is driving, and he seems… happy. Peaceful. This is his happy place. The sun is shining brightly, and we are looking for a place outdoors to hang out by the water for a bit. We used to do this all the time when we were dating. We would load up his giant white Silverado and go looking for an adventure. Camping, hiking, skiing. It didn't really matter what we were doing as long as we were outside and having fun. Those moments have been few and far between since we got married four years ago and started trying for a baby and house hunting right away. Life seems to have gotten in the way of our adventures.

But not today. Today is perfect. I raise my face toward the sun, my eyes closed. The sun feels healing on my face. I breathe deeply, allowing the fresh air to nourish my lungs and my being. Conversation flows easily between me and Troy, which is a welcome change from our typical bickering and disagreements. I feel grounded and calm, awaiting our perfect adventure which is simply on its way to us.

The messages from the etheric realm have not stopped since I met Josette, which at this point, has been several days. In this moment, I notice they are still flowing toward me full force, and I ask my guides to slow down, to allow me to enjoy my humanness and this beautiful moment with my family. After a minute or so, the flow of information begins to feel less like river rapids and more like a gentle, babbling brook. I sigh in relief as I allow myself to be present with my family.

Troy turns off the main road and onto a bumpy gravel road, driving deeper into the woods. He points to the river at our left, "Maybe we can find a good spot off of this river." After several minutes, he pulls over to the side of the road, puts the car in park, and turns off the engine. "This might be a good spot. I'll scope it out with Sampson first."

"Okay, sounds good," I reply, looking around and breathing in the fresh air. After a few minutes, he returns.

"Yeah, this looks good. You want to see before we take Finn out?"

"No, it's okay," I say, trusting his assessment. *I feel so grounded. Joyful. Present,* I think to myself, continuing to feel grateful for the pause.

I climb out of the truck and pull Finn out of his car seat. "Yay! Mama! Trees!" Finn exclaims. He's so similar to Troy in this way. He loves being outside, being in nature. This is a beautiful sight for him. He stomps after Troy and Sampson, who have already begun walking on the short trail to the water.

I keep a close eye on Finn as we approach the water. As I see the river, I feel anxiety begin to rise in my belly and my chest. I reach out and grab Finn. "Hold on, honey... not too fast. Be careful... we have to make safe choices."

"Yeah, safe," Finn repeats back. "Caaaareful, Mama." His reaction pulls me out of my anxious trance for a moment. *This isn't like me,*

I think. *I haven't felt this afraid for Finn's safety since I entered this state of total awareness. This isn't me… at least, not the current me. Where is this coming from?*

You are adjusting. Guidance from the etheric realm begins to flood toward me, anchoring me. *You are experiencing the spiritual realm, and you are experiencing your humanness. This is the 'up, down.' You are experiencing both at once, and both are very intense right now, far apart. You are balancing and acclimating. It won't always feel so far apart, so intense.*

I gently place Finn down and he runs ahead of me again toward Troy and Sampson. *He's so free here,* I think. *I don't want him to be afraid of the world. I want him to experience it.*

Your anxiety is still a part of you. You will learn to heal it, but it takes time. Allow yourself to be present, to be here now with your family.

I take a deep breath and continue walking, and I gasp as the river comes into full view. The cloudless sky overhead allows the sun to shine brightly onto the water, making the river seem like a flowing sheet of diamonds, shimmering brilliantly as it reflects the light back. The trees sway gently in the summer breeze, and the air smells crisp and fresh. I am taken aback by the beauty of it all.

It is not far to the other side, and I notice Troy is already beginning to walk in the water. "I want to see how deep it is," he says. Sampson bounds after him, happily splashing in the water directly behind Troy.

"Okay, just be careful please. It looks like it speeds up a bit toward the middle."

Troy laughs. "This is nothing. It's fine."

I watch him carefully as I hold Finn tightly. *Breathe,* I hear my guides say. I take in a deep breath and blow it out. I chuckle as I see Finn do the same. I feel my grip on Finn loosen a bit as Troy emerges on the other side. The water never reached his knees at its deepest, but as I look down the river a bit, I see the water grow darker.

It gets deeper down the way a bit, I think.

Breathe, my guides repeat. They are working overtime to help me stay grounded.

I hold Finn tightly as I walk into the water, following the same path that Troy took as much as I can. This fear, this hypervigilance… it is a trauma response. Years and years of experiencing the world as unsafe helped create a little girl who eventually grew up to feel as though danger was always right around the corner. This hypervigilance was amplified by having a child, which constantly reminds me that I truly have control over nothing. It's terrifying and anxiety-inducing, and I am feeling it full force right now.

Suddenly, in my mind's eye, I see a flash of my little brother, Lawrence. He drowned in water much shallower than this. The sinking feeling hits my stomach hard, and I quicken my pace to get to the other side of the river. I sigh in relief as I finally emerge from the water and set Finn down, ensuring that I am between him and the river the entire time. *This is torture. I'm so scared.*

Breathe, they respond.

Troy is smiling, throwing rocks into the water. "Come here, Finn!" he says, and Finn starts running toward him. He gets closer and closer to the edge of the river, and I feel panic begin to rise again.

"Please be careful!" I yell. I didn't mean to yell; it's just how it came out. Another flash of Lawrence.

"He's fine!" Troy says back sharply. I pick up on his tone right away and sigh as I catch up to them.

"Sorry… this is just really freaking me out," I say. "Because of Lawrence. It scares me." If Troy heard me, he doesn't show it. I sigh and continue to watch them. They are both happily throwing rocks into the river at this point. I notice that Finn is inching closer and closer to the water.

"It's okay, buddy! Go ahead!" Troy says and Finns smiles up at him approvingly. He looks back at the water and continues to inch toward it.

"I don't like this!" I yell, catching both of them off guard as their gazes snap to me. "The water gets really fast right there! He could get swept up so easily! You're not being careful!"

"You're overreacting. I'm right here," Troy responds, seeming to be confused by my outburst. "I would never let anything happen to him."

I take a deep breath, willing my anxiety to dissipate. *This is torture. You're safe. Your family is safe. Be here now.*

This is so hard. Why is this so hard? I thought I was healing. I feel as though I'm pleading for answers at this point.

Be here now, they repeat. I close my eyes and sigh, bringing my face toward the sun again. I feel the warm rays on my skin and feel the anxiety begin to melt away as I inhale sharply, filling my lungs with fresh breath that quickly seems to make its way to every cell in my body.

I want to be here... I am here... I say to myself as I imagine my anxiety dissipating and floating away. When I open my eyes, I see Finn happily splashing in the water, which is now up to his waist. Troy is on the other side of him, ensuring that he stands between him and the rest of the river.

He's so free in the water. He loves it.

He can only be present to the extent that you allow him to be, they say. *You must model it for him. He won't be able to be present otherwise. He will always be looking to you for safety. If you do not surrender to this present moment, neither will he.*

But my anxiety, I continue. *It makes it so difficult.*

Your body will adjust. You must give it time, they reply. *Be here now.*

Thank you, I say to them, my anxiety mostly gone at this point. I take one more deep breath and run into the river to meet my boys.

10

COMPROMISES

It is now evening and both Finn and Troy are fast asleep. I am sitting in a bath with lavendar-infused Epsom salts, pondering the truths that have been revealed to me not just earlier today but over the last few days. Currently, I am contemplating the notion of systems and the world as we currently know it. Humans have created so many constructs over the centuries, the millennia, to attempt to bring order and control to our existence. As I process, my spirit guides begin to show me images using pop culture. One is the movie, *The Matrix*. Neo is not Neo in the matrix. He is Thomas Anderson, software programmer for a large corporation. *The matrix… that's what this all is,* I say to myself. The constructs that we have all bought into—working corporate jobs for security, money as a false idol—none of it actually exists. It is all energy, and energy is the underlying current in our world, this ordinary reality.

That is correct. Money doesn't exist. A voice says in my mind, no doubt one of my spirit guides.

Okay, so… if money doesn't exist, then what? What do I do with that information? I still need money to survive, to feed my family… I don't understand… I reply, trying to read the message between the lines.

Money doesn't exist, but money is a tool.

Money is a tool. Of course, I repeat to myself.

In an effort to help me understand, my guides send me an image in my mind's eye. I'm in a kitchen, but it is not our house. It is bigger and more updated. Airy and light. Beautiful. The energy is gorgeous and peaceful. I'm standing in the kitchen, drinking a glass of water, and talking to... a chef? I'm laughing and deep in a conversation as the chef cuts vegetables. I put the glass in the sink and begin rummaging through a drawer. I'm clearly looking for something. *Is this... my house?* I ask. I'm met with a mental nod. I continue to look around. *Wow...* I say, awestruck. *It's incredible...*

I'm not much older than I am now. The vision feels maybe one or two years away, at most. I look around. It's a beautifully updated kitchen with white contemporary cabinets and a stone countertop on a large island. I look to the left and there is a breakfast nook with a small table, cozy chairs tucked away in front of large windows, and sheer curtains swaying in the breeze. The air smells fragrant, a gentle blend of salt water and sunshine. I get an intuitive sense that I live on the coast.

This home... how is it... I have a chef? I say, incredulously. I see my guides chuckle, teasingly.

And a housekeeper. And a gardener, they add. *You have built a community here, and they all love you. They love working for you. You pour love into them, and, in turn, they pour love into everything they do for you and Finn.*

And Troy... I say absently, still admiring my gorgeous kitchen. They do not reply.

Instead of acknowledging my last comment, they say: *You will make a lot of money very soon.* I instinctively cringe.

I mean... that's nice, I guess... one less thing to worry about, right? I reply. *But if I'm trying to be in service of Source, how am I supposed to become...* I swallow, feeling the gut in my stomach, and continue, *rich? Wealthy? Shouldn't I be charging LESS for what I do, not MORE, if this is truly Source-led work?*

Money is a tool, they say. *Right now, money affords access to influence, impact... a platform to get a message out. You are a messenger. You will make money doing good work, the work you chose to do here in this specific life. You will make money doing that work which will enable you more access to more people. You have a message to convey. You will have a large audience which will also generate income. And then you will find ways to redistribute your wealth equitably.*

Suddenly, I am transported to another time and place. I am in our present house, but it is empty. I see our realtor walking me and Troy throughout the house, noting positive features and areas of concern.

"You could do a pretty decent remodel for around $20K," she says, pointing at the dark, 60s-style cabinets in the kitchen. "You will want to take out this wall, make this an island," she pats the countertop. "It can be done, but it's always tougher after you move in."

I look over at Troy. "I... I want a kitchen, a decent one," I say, remembering why it was so important to me. The kitchen is the heart of a Filipino home. We had been talking about trying for a baby for several months and recently officially began trying. This baby was energetically and spiritually on its way, and I knew I would spend a lot of time in the kitchen. I just wanted it to be beautiful and welcoming. I wanted it to be big and allow for several people to be in the kitchen at the same time. Filipinos have a hard time staying out of the kitchen, and I love that. I wanted a space that invited that sort of community, especially if I was going to spend a lot of time in there postpartum.

Troy opens the outdated, solid wood cupboards and looks inside, continuing to examine the space. "Updating the kitchen wouldn't be a priority to me," he says. "I just want us to get into a house before the baby arrives."

"Troy, it's the one thing I really want," I say, feeling sad and frustrated all at once. I continue to argue, but I sense my voice blending into the background, sounding further and further away. *I'm disappearing*, I think to myself in this present moment.

"We can always worry about it later," he says. "Right now, we need a house. We need to be somewhere we can receive a child in."

I sigh, exasperated. This house hunt has been riddled with anxiety and disappointment, mostly Troy's. He is hell-bent on being in a house as soon as our child arrives, and I sense that he is prioritizing that security over finding the house that is truly *ours*. I feel as though I have said my piece multiple times, and it doesn't do any good. He charges ahead anyway. In this moment, I choose not to stand in his way. I have found that it is difficult to continue to challenge him, especially when his anxiety is at play. We decide to put an offer in on the house.

When did I stop asking for what I need? I ask my guides, tears forming in my eyes.

This is the way it often went in all of your relationships, my guides respond quietly, gently holding space for my emotions that are coming forward. A sequence of dissolved friendships and romantic relationships surface to the forefront of my awareness. They show me the relationships before they ended. *Before you let go of people,* they say, *especially those you care deeply about, you have the tendency to lose yourself. You are incredibly loyal. It takes a lot for you to walk away.*

Another image enters my awareness. I am in college, lying on my couch in the apartment that I shared with my boyfriend at the time, Ty. We had a small 1-bedroom apartment in a new construction high rise on the Tacoma waterfront, within walking distance of my college. It is nighttime and I am crying.

That's the night, I say, head cocked. *That's the night I had the dream.*

Yes, my guides respond. Ty had been angry at me. We got into a big fight about Owen, a guy that I was seeing prior to dating him. Owen had had a girlfriend when we were sleeping together, and now, about a year later, Ty was berating me about how I could possibly date him, especially if he had a girlfriend. He didn't care about him having a girlfriend, though. That wasn't the real issue. Ty was incredibly jealous and possessive, and we worked side-by-side with a guy who had seen me naked. He had *had* me, and Ty was obsessed with me. He had admitted at one point that he was *consumed* by me.

"I… was sad and lonely," I had replied quietly, feeling the overwhelming need to explain my behavior, even though I had been seeing Owen well before Ty and I began dating. "My brother had just died and I was sad…"

"Ugh! God, Lani…," he spat the words, disgusted. "Don't use your brother's death as an excuse for being a whore." He stormed into our bedroom and slammed the door. I knew what that meant—I was sleeping on the couch.

I lie on my couch sobbing. My breathing slows down after a moment, and I drift off to sleep. In my dream state, I see a circle of people gathering around a small figure. As I approach the circle, I see my little brother who had been almost 2 years old when he drowned. He is standing at the center of the circle and people are patting his back, smiling and talking with him excitedly.

"Lawrence?" I say in disbelief. "Is it really you?" Somehow, I know it is truly him and not just the dream version of him. *This wasn't a dream*, I say to my guides, and I sense nodding. *This was a vision. I journeyed to meet my brother that night.*

I reach down to pick him up, and I feel the rolls of his arms and legs. "It *is* you!" I say, crying and laughing, "I miss you so much…" I hug him tightly.

He looks up at me, smiling, then his face turns stern. He places his hand on my cheek. *Ate...* he says telepathically. *What are you doing, Ate? You're stronger than this... You know you deserve better than how he is treating you. It's time to leave...* The vision ends, and he is gone. I am back in my apartment, lying on my couch, my face and pillow damp with tears.

The next day, I pack a bag and leave Ty.

That was the first time, I say. *It's the first time I connected with the spirit realm to receive a message. It was my first vision.*

Not the first time, they say. *But it's one of the most pivotal. It's the first time in your adult life that you began to trust your spiritual gifts.*

I sigh, reflecting on the images they had just shown me. *So, I guess it looks like I'm going to be making much more money soon...* I say, still processing. *And money is a tool. I will use money to amplify this message. And...* I struggle to find the tie to the relationship message. *I have been playing small. And sometimes...*

Sometimes you need us, they say. *To guide you, to steer you. This current life, for you, has been so tumultuous... so traumatic... that you will stay in situations much longer than you need to. Jobs. Relationships. Friendships. 'We accept the love we think we deserve...'* My mind goes to that quote, my favorite line from the book *The Perks of Being a Wallflower*. It continues to feel interesting to me that they use pop culture to communicate with me, to help me make instant connections.

Okay. Okay, I trust you, I respond after considering their words. *Can you just do one thing for me?*

What's that?

Please just make it clear, I say, *if I need to leave.*

Of course, they respond. And then they are gone.

11

THE CAVE

The following day, I gently close the door to Finn's room after putting him down for his nap. These couple of hours in the middle of the day are my and Troy's only reprieve from having to juggle working full-time and caring for him, so I try to make the most of it.

On this particular day, I find myself drawn to quiet solitude. I close my office door gently so as to avoid waking Finn and plop down into my comfy office chair. I take a deep breath and cross my legs, allowing my hands to fall gently onto my knees, palms up.

My breathing slows and I begin to make out an image in my mind's eye: a giant meadow speckled with purple and yellow wildflowers, snow-capped mountains far in the distance. I see a body of water in the distance and begin moving toward it. The water is sparkling on the surface, beckoning me forward. It looks deep, and I feel a tinge of fear. *Jump,* my guides say, and I do.

I do not dive headfirst like so many people can do gracefully. I jump in feet first and feeling somewhat afraid. *Why does this feel so real?* I ask.

What is real? Is this not real? I hear my guides respond.

The words echo in my mind as I begin moving my arms and legs, swimming deeper and deeper into the water. I begin to panic as the light from the surface begins to fade to darkness. Deeper and deeper.

I can breathe, I assure myself. *I can breathe underwater.* This feeling, this assurance is not something that is foreign to me. I find myself having to tell myself this in dreams. Drowning is always a deep-seated fear of mine until I remind myself that I can breathe. I'm safe.

The sun is now invisible and I'm surrounded by nothingness, darkness. A brief moment of panic washes over me. *I can breathe.* I continue to swim deeper and deeper.

Suddenly, I notice a small light, barely visible. I squint to try to make it out as I swim closer and closer to it. The closer I get to the light, the brighter and bigger it becomes. *It's a cave,* I say to myself. I swim harder and harder until I finally reach it. The inside of the cave is completely dry, and I look behind me at the water from which I emerged. The water looks like a sheet of glass, unmoving. *The veil,* I think instinctively.

The light has dimmed to a dull glow, and I begin to look around. I see a large Kermode bear (or spirit bear), a poised bald eagle, a small family of rabbits, and my beloved dog, Patches, who passed away several years ago. These animals have all meant something significant to me in my life. They have presented themselves to me at various times and provided unspoken guidance when I have needed it the most. Bears have always been a part of my life, and they represent me at my core: fierce protector, hibernator, caretaker. The eagle represents my yearning to be free as well as my visionary instincts. Rabbits arrived when Troy and I were considering trying for our first child, representing fertility and family. Patches helped me heal when I was processing my childhood trauma; he was the only one who saw me in my lowest of lows.

Why are you all here? I ask, being careful to convey the reverence I feel being in their presence. *Do you have a message for me?*

Yes, they say in one collective voice. *It is time to heal, to move forward. It is time to integrate and to stand firmly in your truth. We are all different parts of you, and we are all separate for now. Integration is required.*

How do I do that?

You will know, they reply. *You are wiser than you are allowing yourself to believe. The answers reside within you. All you have to do is be present and listen. Know that you are capable. Know that you are loved. Know that you have everything you need to fulfill your mission. We are always with you.*

They all bow to me, and I instinctively bow back. They make their way back through the veil and into the deep waters, all swimming in different directions. I try to follow, but by the time I pass through the veil and enter the water, they are gone.

I swim back to the surface, climb out of the water, and lie down on my back in the field of wildflowers. I watch the clouds pass overhead for a few moments before I take a deep breath and open my eyes to reengage with the present moment.

12

LETTING GO

It's bedtime, and I'm watching Finn pull books off of his bookshelf. He is trying to choose one for us to read together before he settles down for bed.

I'm so grateful, I say to my guides. *He is teaching me so much. I truly believe I have more to learn from him than he has to learn from me.*

Finn pulls a book off the shelf and grins, holding it up. "Good egg!" he exclaims proudly, holding up the book *The Good Egg* with both hands. I smile as he climbs onto my lap.

He is so attuned to the spiritual world, I continue telling my guides as I begin to read the book aloud. *He is an open channel and freely communicates with me telepathically. I think I will become a better channel by being his mother. I just need to find a way to allow him to guide me… to not get so caught up in things being the way I imagine them in my mind. I want to be less attached to outcomes and more open to the way that he sees things going. I think he could guide me toward being the best channel I can be in this life…*

My mind continues to drift as I realize that Finn is beginning to fidget in my lap. "What is it, honey?" I ask, setting the book down for a moment. "Are you okay?"

Suddenly, he lets out a piercing scream and begins to flail his arms around. He went from being calm and subdued to completely miserable in an instant. He jumps off of my lap and plops down onto the floor, completely irate. I sit down on the floor next to him, feeling quite helpless.

"What's going on, buddy? Are you sad? Are you mad?"

He doesn't even acknowledge my questions and continues to scream, now pounding his fists on the ground. I am completely flabbergasted by the outburst and quite unsure of what to do. Troy appears in the doorway.

"What's wrong?" he asks, and I shrug.

"I have no idea. He just started freaking out." I feel panic begin to rise within me. I can typically track him pretty easily, understand his outbursts and moods. This is different. I have no idea what is happening with him, and it terrifies me.

"Buddy, what is it? Do you want some snacks?" Troy asks, genuinely trying to help. Finn doesn't acknowledge him either.

"It's okay," I sigh. "I'm just going to sit with him for a bit." Troy closes the door, and I can hear the sound of his footsteps fade as he walks away.

Suddenly, Ky comes to mind. She and Finn have been connecting deeply lately. Yesterday, Finn drew a picture and, when I sent it to Ky, she was taken aback. "That's exactly like a drawing I just did a couple of months ago… the circles, the lines, the dots… he's picking up on my energy."

Maybe she will know what's going on… how I can help him… I think to myself as I pick up my phone to call her.

"Hey Auntie Lani," she greets me. "What's up?"

"Finn is really upset," I say, sounding a bit more panicked than I intended. My anxiety continues to creep up, and I feel that something is seriously wrong. "I think… I think Finn is trying to communicate something to me. Can you tell what is going on?

Are you able to connect with him?"

"Sure, give me a sec…," the line goes quiet for about a minute. Finn's sobs begin to slow and eventually quiet. I watch in amazement as he catches his breath and his sobs fade away. He looks around, picks up another book, and begins to walk over to me. I pick myself up and sit back down in his rocker, allowing him to gently climb onto my lap. "So…," Ky starts again, "you have to let him go."

"Wait, what?" I ask, genuinely confused. My mind races as I desperately try to understand what that could possibly mean. "What do you mean let him go?"

She pauses, undoubtedly considering her words. "We were under a willow tree, the two of us talking. You were down the hill a bit."

The image materializes easily in my mind's eye as she describes it. "Yeah… yeah, I see it," I reply.

"You couldn't hear us talking because there's something you're not meant to know. At least, not yet," she says. I trust her assessment and continue to listen. "But he says that you have been leaning too heavily on him to teach you how to channel, how to be a spiritual being on Earth. You have to let him go."

Tears sting my eyes as the weight of her words begin to make sense to me. She continues, "You have to let him be a kid, live his life. He can't be your teacher because he needs a mom right now, not someone to teach. You have to… you have to let him back through the veil. He can't stay on this side with you. He's not meant to."

My face is hot with emotion as I feel tears fall from my eyes. *Grief. This is grief.* I can feel arms around me… my spirit guides. They are holding me. They know this is a tough lesson.

"You have to let him go. He needs to have a human experience. He's not meant to stay on this side of the veil his whole life. None of us are. We can make our way back eventually, but we can't live a full life on this side of the veil. We need to fully experience humanness, ego. You have to let him go. You have to let him be a kid." Ky's voice has become quiet and soothing at this point, no doubt to counteract the devastating sadness she senses on my end.

"So…" I choke out the word, still gathering my thoughts and what I am trying to convey. "I have to… sit back and watch him move back through the veil, back toward his humanness? Back toward… suffering? How am I supposed to do that… how could I possibly allow that? I can't…"

"You can," Ky gently cuts me off, her voice even. Comforting. "This is his journey. He's not meant to stay on this side of the veil. He needs to learn lessons; he needs to experience heartache. He needs to… feel human. You have to let him go, Auntie Lani."

I let out an audible cry, tears now flowing quickly and heavily. "I love you, Auntie Lani," I hear Ky say quietly into the phone.

"I love you, too… I should go…," I say in between loud sobs. I look down at Finn, who has completely calmed down at this point. He is sitting in my lap, holding a book, and gently flipping through the pages.

"Okay… okay, bye," she says with a touch of hesitancy in her voice. I sense that she wants to comfort me and to assure me that I will be okay, but I also sense that she received guidance on her end that she needs to let me sit with the information. I hear a click and the phone goes silent.

I continue to look down at Finn, noting again how peaceful he seems now, and I squeeze him tightly. *I don't want to let him go… this is so hard…* I plead with my guides. I sense their support as I continue to hold him, swaying from side to side. After a few more moments, I turn off the light and gently lay him down on his bed. I cover him with a blanket and stroke his hair until he falls asleep.

***

In the morning, I see a video message from my friend, Grace. I smile faintly as I see her image surface in my mind's eye: her gently tussled wavy blonde hair, light skin, and soft expression. It never seems to matter what time of day it is, she always seems to look radiant. Exchanging video messages from Grace has become a daily occurrence, and, honestly, some days, it is the only thing that keeps me going. I feel comforted knowing that across town, someone can still see me so clearly and be an advocate and supporter of my process.

Grace and I met in grad school about ten years ago. We were in the same MBA program and fell into a deep friendship quickly and were inseparable for a time. We connected effortlessly around our shared joy and love of life. She was a breath of fresh air at a time in my life of deep transformation and growth. During the first year of our friendship, I moved out of the home I had built with my long-term boyfriend, moved into a place of my own, struggled through my first year of my MBA, and traveled with her and several other grad school friends to the Dolomites for a leadership course abroad. During that year, I also dived headfirst into examining my childhood sexual trauma which triggered a deep depression and anxiety within me that had been lying dormant for years while simultaneously informing literally every relationship I engaged in.

During that time, there were days on end when I could not find the strength to shower, let alone leave my apartment to engage with others or even go to work or school. Grace and I lived about a mile apart in West Seattle; she became a consistent source of support during that time, suggesting that we meet often for walks, runs, and yoga classes. She listened to me deeply as I conveyed all of the ways in which my trauma was showing up in my life and held space for my healing in ways that my soul craved at the time. She provided me a sense of community that I never received from people outside of my immediate family.

In this present moment, Grace has also been going through a process of transformation and awakening as well. I guided her through the veil recently, and she has been consistently leaning into her own divinity since then. I had sent her a message first thing in the morning explaining the events of the evening prior. I was able to explain it to her through heavy sobs, still feeling the grief of the moment even hours later.

"Hi friend," Grace starts, her face showing concern, no doubt still processing the message she just received from me. "I'm so sad to hear about that. How absolutely devastating... heartbreaking. The thought that is occurring to me right now is... that you cannot save everyone. Even with all of your spiritual gifts and support from the etheric realm... you just can't. And you're not meant to. And that must feel so... SO hard..."

Tears fall from my eyes and run down my cheeks as her words penetrate my being. I know it's true, and it's one of the hardest truths I've had to accept to date.

"The tears that you are shedding," she continues, "I think those are tears for humanity. To be human is to know suffering. And try as you may, you cannot save everyone from their suffering. And I think it would just be so difficult to know that... that you can't save even those you care the most about. It's heartbreaking to know... that you can't save those you love..."

I am transported back to my earliest memory, when I was a small infant in my crib, reaching for my mother. All this time, I was sure I was crying since she wouldn't pick me up. I thought *I* was suffering.

No. I had it all wrong.

I was reaching out to soothe my mother. She was suffering, and I sensed that I could help. I could ease her suffering, if she would only let me. I cried so that she would pick me up, so that I could heal her.

I chose to be here... Awareness continues to dawn on me as I process the memory. *I chose to be here at this particular point in human history... to help. That's my purpose and that's my mission: to help. And the fact that I can't save everyone is... unbearable.*

Your mission is to help, my guides reply gently. *But it's not to save humanity. You alone cannot do that. You're not meant to.*

POSSIBILITIES

"I have something to tell you…," I say to Troy, working up the courage to share more of my experience with him.

"What's up?" he says, putting his phone down. It is late afternoon, and we are both done working. We have a couple of hours before the hustle of dinner and bedtime begins. It's generally the only time we really have to connect on the weekdays; although, admittedly, we rarely use the time as such. Juggling work and parenting responsibilities during COVID has left us both completely depleted, and we usually veg out during this time. I know I am making a risky choice broaching this subject right now.

"So… you know how I have told you I have a connection to the spiritual realm? That I can actually *hear spirits* sometimes?" I see him move his body uncomfortably. I know he doesn't believe that my reality is possible, but he has told me in the past that he believes that *I believe* that it is happening for me. Which, honestly, is not conducive to creating a safe space for me to share my recent experiences with him. I proceed despite what I know: that this will, most likely, not be received well.

"Sure," he responds halfheartedly, and I can already sense his attention wavering.

"Well," I continue, "I think that the spiritual realm is telling me to begin putting more energy into my business. I think I need to focus on coaching and…," I brace myself for his reaction. "I am supposed to write a book."

"Oh, hm…," he says, and although I can sense he is genuinely trying to appear supportive and interested, I can feel the intensity of his fear creeping up in his body as if it were my own fear. "Do you think… now is the best time to make a shift like that? I mean, more and more people are losing their jobs every day. There is so much uncertainty with COVID…"

I stop to consider his words and formulate my response. *I'm so tired of having to use rationale to explain things to him… rationale has no place here.*

And… my guides respond, *you must find ways to get messages across so that people in this current construct can hear them. You are a translator. You can find the data. You can find the words. Allow us to speak through you.* I take a deep breath to consider their words and allow their words through.

"There is uncertainty in my corporate job, too," I reply. "People are being laid off left and right. I think it's just a matter of time before I am on the chopping block as well. I honestly think this is a prudent choice, and I don't think that staying in my corporate job is any more secure than building my business." I went on to describe how the diversity, equity, and inclusion field is booming right now.

"So, are you thinking of quitting your job, is that what you're saying?"

"Not necessarily," I say. "But I do want to consider it as a possibility, especially because I think this is my path. This is what has been laid out before me…" My guides advise me to pause so as not to lose him.

"I don't know," Troy says warily. "It seems irrational right now to do anything drastic." He continues to shift uncomfortably and cross and uncross his arms.

"I understand," I say, feeling a bit defeated. Just then, my guides show me a vision of the life that Troy, Finn, and I would live if I took this path right now. I smile as I sense exactly where they want me to go next. "Well, I'm going to write this book, and I have a really strong feeling that it will be important and a lot of people will read it. Wouldn't it be cool if this is what changed everything, if we just became rich after this?" I know that much of Troy's fear stems from his insecurity around money, so it makes sense to me that my guides are encouraging me to speak this way, even though it makes me uncomfortable.

"Well, yeah, of course!" he says, a small smile reaching his lips. "But it's not something to bank on. It's so risky."

"Okay, okay, I get that. But Troy…," I start, continuing to interpret the messages that my guides are sending me. "Can you just dream with me for a moment?"

He sighs deeply before agreeing. "Sure."

"So… let's just pretend that this book is really popular and a lot of people read it. Let's say that I write more and more books and, over the course of the next few years, we find that we don't need to work anymore, at least not in the traditional sense. What would you want to do?"

"I mean," he looks up, contemplatively. "I wouldn't want to do anything." He chuckles.

I grin. "Well, okay. Fair enough. But I do believe we would want to travel. And if I'm solely a full-time writer, we don't really need to stay in one place for too long. What if we just traveled the world? Stayed in one place for a month or two then moved on?"

"Well, that would be amazing!" he says, his eyes beaming. I feel excited in this moment. *We're dreaming together…*

"I mean, I would probably need your help planning the trips and where we were going… booking Airbnb's, etc…"

"Oh, I could totally do that. I like doing that," he replies, grinning from ear to ear.

I walk over to him and sit on his lap and wrap my arms around his neck. "We could go to the Philippines and stay with my dad for a couple of months… Fiji… we could go wherever we wanted. It feels so freeing, doesn't it?"

"Yeah, that would be pretty amazing…," his voice drifts off, and I can tell that his notion of reality is beginning to sink back in. He is starting to consider how implausible this all truly is.

"Thanks for dreaming with me, babe," I say preemptively, before he has a chance to refute the possibility of this actually being our reality. I kiss him on the lips before I stand up and walk away, smiling.

14

REMEMBERING

"Okay, Ky. I have to run to this akashic records training. Wish me luck!"

"Yes!!" Ky says and I can sense her smiling broadly. "I'm excited for you! Good luck... I can't wait to be your guinea pig!"

I chuckle as I say goodbye and end the phone call. It is Saturday, and I have been looking forward to this first training session all week. I allow my mind to wander as I search my email for the virtual meeting invite from Carla, the spiritual teacher who will be training me on how to access the akashic records. I am transported to the first time I heard about the records from my dear friend and Reiki practitioner, Meesa, several months prior. I had been trying to figure out what the next skill was that I wanted to learn, essentially adding it to my spiritual toolbox.

"I am not sure what I'm supposed to learn next," I had said, "but I feel like it has something to do with energy. Maybe Reiki?"

"Hm...," I heard Meesa say on the other end of the phone. "I don't know about that."

"What do you mean?" I say, puzzled. I thought she would be excited to hear that I was interested in studying Reiki.

"Well," she continued, "I am thinking about your connection with the spiritual realm, and I always imagined you learning something like accessing the akashic records."

"Accessing the aka—what?" I said, genuinely confused. "I have no idea what you just said. What is that?"

"Akashic records," she said with a small laugh. "I swear, for a spiritual being, you're such an infant sometimes!"

"Look, bish…," I respond, laughing. Flipping shit back and forth to each other was sign of affection in our friendship. "Just tell me what it is!"

"It's basically a system, a structure," she explained. "It's a way to access the data from all of our *other* lives and dimensions in order to obtain information to help us on our soul's journey, here in this lifetime."

My voice caught in my throat before I found it again and responded. "Wait, what?! How does that exist? That sounds amazing! I can learn how to do that?"

"I'll connect you with my girl, Jerylle. She's an akashic records practitioner and can give you more information. Maybe even connect you with a teacher."

My awareness abruptly comes back to the present moment, as I enter the virtual meeting room with Carla. We exchange pleasantries and I suddenly sense fear and anxiety creeping up in my torso.

"Carla, I have to be honest…," I say, feeling the need to be forthright. "I have this sinking feeling that I'm not going to be very good at this. I'm finding more and more that I am not a super structured person, so the thought of engaging with a structure to access spiritual information seems like something I may not be very good at. Like, maybe I'm too unstructured to tap into the etheric realm this way, too 'go-with-the-flow' to do it right."

I think back to the first akashic records reading I ever had with Meesa's connection, Jerylle. I was amazed at her commitment to ritual. She recited prayers and mantras in order to open the records, ask questions and seek clarification, gather information, and close the records. It felt dreamy, and it also felt like a lot of work. And so structured.

"What if I don't remember the mantras, the prayers? What if I miss a word? What if I open the wrong records?"

Carla smiles gently, which reminds me of the way Josette smiled back at me when my anxiety had crept up in our first virtual meeting. I feel my shoulders relax and drop.

"I know you are powerful," she starts. "That is something we talked about when we met for the first time. This work is all about having a pure intention when you enter the records, and to be really honest, there's no 'wrong way' to do it as long as you are accessing the records for the right reasons."

I feel my body begin to relax further as I listen to her process. *She sounds a lot like me,* I think to myself. She does not buy into the notion that there has to be a lot of rigidity and a lot of structure around how the records are accessed. She also believes that everyone can have a different process and still get the information they are meant to receive.

"We will walk through the manual together, which is basically just something to refer back to, if needed. It can also provide a bit more structure to those wanting it," she says. "However, your process of accessing the records will likely be completely different than anyone else's. I will guide you through it and support you in finding your unique process."

I sigh in relief. "Okay, that sounds great. Thank you for clarifying that!"

Carla spends the next hour or so walking me through the manual, offering prayers and mantras for reference but assuring me that I can find my own way. Her energy is calming, completely accepting of who I am. I continue to melt into the process.

"Okay, are you ready to access your records?" she asks. At this point, she has completely put me at ease.

"Yes!" I reply excitedly, and my response is genuine.

"Wonderful! I invite you to close your eyes..." she begins. As I listen to her gentle instructions, my body begins to feel heavy. "Allow your breath to fill your lungs... gently exhale..."

In this moment, I feel completely rooted, my human body seemingly grounded in the Earth, while my consciousness simultaneously floats above me. It is a feeling that is familiar to me, something that happens to me often during meditations. However, it has never happened so quickly, almost instantaneously. I focus on her words.

"Now... allow yourself to enter the records. Begin to take note of how it looks. This is what we discussed... about allowing the space to reveal itself to you..."

Carla had mentioned earlier in the call that when she is entering the records, she imagines a large orb in front of her filled with shimmering star dust. Once she enters the records, she gets information quickly, like an intuitive *knowing*. It's not something she has to seek out. It just arrives in her consciousness.

In my mind's eye, I imagine the orb she had described. I attempt to enter it, but I have trouble. *This isn't for me,* I think as I continue to relax my body. *This isn't mine...*

Suddenly, I begin to see people materialize in front of me. As I continue to breathe deeply and my muscles continue to relax, the image begins to take shape even further. I am in the middle of a bustling, outdoor market. The streets in front of me are lined on both sides with vendors behind carts and kiosks. I am reminded of the fresh fish and vegetable markets in the Philippines. Or perhaps vendors lining the streets of the Vatican. It was both markets and neither all at once. Every single outdoor market in the world even and simultaneously none that currently exist in the physical realm. I continue to look around and notice that I am at an intersection. In each of the four directions I look, I see vendors stretching for miles and miles. Infinity. There is no beginning to the market and there is no end. And I can be at the whole market all at once. It is all so fascinating.

I describe the image I'm seeing to Carla, and she asks, "How are you feeling? How does it feel to be here?"

"It feels like home," I respond. "I feel accepted, seen. Understood."

"Beautiful. What do you feel called to do next? Do you feel called to talk to anyone?"

Just then, I notice a woman coming toward me. While most people in the center of the streets are milling about, some seeming to move with purpose, some seeming incredibly confused and out-of-place, she is the only person in the entire market making eye contact with me. Her pace quickens as she nears me and a grin spreads across her face. I ask her who she is and respond out loud to Carla.

"Joan of Arc. She's one of my spirit guides. Is that even her name here in this realm?"

"Why don't you ask her?"

"What would you like me to call you?" I say out loud, waiting for a response. "V... Venus... Hm. Okay." Now she is crying, wiping away happy tears, as she places her hands on my shoulders. She is so grateful, so glad to see me. She hugs me tightly, and I welcome the embrace. *You're here! You're finally here!* I hear her say. *You're home.*

"Does she have anything for you? An offering? A message?" asks Carla.

I see her holding out a heart, glowing bright red in her hands, as she begins to lift it toward me. She continues to bring it higher, mirroring where my heart resides in my chest. I feel my body tense up as I notice her attempting to place it into my body, perhaps to merge with my own heart, and I laugh as she begins to get very animated as she tries to shove the glowing heart toward me. She is now putting her entire body behind the effort and says to me, *Would you just let me love you?*

I relax and watch as the heart finally melts into my body; it moves around a bit before settling into the space. But I still notice a small portion of my heart that is gray and has not quite transformed to the bright red color. *Now, it's time to love yourself,* she says.

I continue to describe what I am seeing and hearing to Carla, but she, as well as the rest of the human realm, crumbles and gently falls away as I continue to focus on the market and Venus. Suddenly, Carla's voice is now in my mind, seemingly no longer as a voice I am hearing in the physical realm. Her voice and my voice are the same now. I can no longer tell where she ends and where I begin. We are connected on this journey, transcending time and space for this specific message.

What else are you seeing? Where shall we go next?

I briefly look around, suddenly aware of the fact that Carla and Venus are both with me now in the market, but they are trailing me. They are trusting me to guide us to whatever is next on this journey.

The vendors are piquing my interest… I turn to my right and look inquisitively at a man behind a cart. He looks older, perhaps in his fifties, and his features are dark. He seems to be of middle eastern descent, and he is expressionless under a thick, dark beard. I look down at the items on his cart, and I am surprised to see nothing but blurred shapes. I focus, relaxing my mind to encourage something to come through. Yet, I am still unable to make out the items, unable to comprehend what they are.

These are not for me, are they? I ask him. A small smile forms underneath his beard as he shakes his head.

No, he responds softly.

I turn and look around again, up and down the streets of the market. The streets stretch for miles and miles until they are out of sight. As I continue to take note of my surroundings, I begin to notice something glowing warm red in the distance. I walk in that direction and see that it is another vendor's cart. As I approach, I notice a woman standing behind the cart. She has long, flowing dark brown hair, and I notice tiny white and pink flowers gently placed amongst soft curls. She's wearing a shimmering, golden dress which flows perfectly over the soft curves of her breasts and her hips. The top of the dress has thin straps and I notice her perfect shoulders. She cocks her head to one side as her bright green eyes pierce my spirit in the most loving way possible, a small smile spreading across her heart shaped face as she greets me silently.

She's beautiful, I hear myself say, and I begin to feel self-conscious, a bit shy. I look away, feeling almost blinded by her beauty and the brilliance of her spirit. She has the air of a goddess, someone sent from the divine realm to make me feel small. I feel undeserving of being in the presence of such raw beauty.

As I look down, avoiding her knowing gaze, I see the items on her cart. *More hearts,* I say to myself. This time they are red and white, shimmering, sparkling, glowing, and pearlescent.

Do you know her? I hear Carla say behind me. *Perhaps from another life?*

Suddenly, I am transported to a vision I had of another life. In this vision, which I had originally seen several years ago during a Reiki session, I first see myself as a child. It appears to be some time in the 1400s or so, somewhere in Europe. I know I am of noble blood because I watch myself sneak out of a castle to join the peasants in the village outside of the castle gates. I am laughing, playing, dancing, and eating. I am barefoot in the grass, running through meadows, small white and pink wildflowers adorning my hair. In this same vision, I am transported through time and see myself as a young woman, dressed in an elaborate gold and white dress, pearls affixed in ornate patterns and designs all over, caressing my soft curves. I gaze longingly out the castle window, seeing the peasants outside the castle gates. They are laughing and poking fun at one another. Walking through the streets and greeting one another. Eating and dancing and living their lives. They are free. I am trapped. I think of my two children, whom I love dearly yet are not enough to keep me feeling fulfilled. Purposeful. I think of my loveless marriage and the man who I married out of obligation in order to keep our kingdom from ruin.

Now, as I look into this beautiful woman's vibrant green eyes, the vision begins to have more context. I see myself sneaking out of the castle and meeting her. We are both young girls, children. *She is the reason,* I say to myself in the market. *She is why I am sneaking out. She is who I am meeting.*

I see myself barefoot in the grass, laughing and playing with this striking little girl. I see her delicately placing wildflowers in my hair.

Then, I see myself older, about 18 or 19. We are teenagers, and we are in a stable, lying on a blanket, both of us naked. She is pushing my hair out of my face and leaning in to kiss me. *We're in love,* I say. *We have been in love our whole lives.*

My vision fast-forwards, and I am on my death bed. This goddess… she is holding my hand, urging me with her eyes to let go, to be at peace. She and I had kept up with this affair, this secret romance, our entire lives. And I was taking the secret of our love to my grave. No one had ever known how deeply I loved this woman. No one could know. We both would have been killed.

Suddenly, I notice my human body, the one sitting in front of the computer, eyes closed. I am weeping. *It's heartbreaking. The whole thing. It hurts,* I say. *How could I do that? How could I hide what you meant to me for so long? How could you ever forgive me?*

There is nothing to forgive, she says as we both stand in the market. *You can let go. You have to let go. And it's time for you to start accepting yourself, accepting this part of yourself.* She hands me one of the glowing red hearts, and I watch as it enters my chest, filling even the gray shadows where Venus's heart could not reach. My heart is whole now, glowing bright red.

She then instructs me to connect with her often. I can do so by quieting my mind and asking her to come forward. She will always come. She is here to guide me to self-love and to help me remember how fully I can love. Remind me of how fluid my love is. It cannot be caged.

Thank you... is all I can manage to say before Carla guides me out of the records.

***

It is now evening, and I am settling into a yoga Nidra meditation, making myself comfortable on my bed. I drape the comforter over my body and listen to my instructor's soft voice.

"Now, imagine your inner sanctuary in your mind... this is a place where you feel safe, secure..."

My mind wanders back to the stable, this beautiful goddess and I are wrapped in each other's arms. *She is my safe place, my inner sanctuary...*

All of the sudden, I feel warmth in my legs, the sign of my connecting with the divine realm. The warmth continues up my legs, and I begin to feel warm in my pelvis. I let out a soft moan as I imagine her lips on my body; her fingers are caressing every square inch of my skin. My human body is lying perfectly still in this meditation, and my heart is not racing. Yet, in this safe place, in the depths of my spiritual consciousness, I am wild with ecstasy as she explores my body with hers. For several minutes, I savor the thought, the feeling of her body on mine. I feel myself climbing higher and higher, and I feel a release in my human body as I climax.

I don't question how I was able to climax without even touching myself. Instead, I begin to weep. *I miss you,* I say. *Are you here, in this human realm? Are you nearby? How can I find you?*

These are not answers you need to know just yet, she replies softly, holding me as I drift off to sleep. *Please… just be here with me. Be here now.*

15

SHEDDING

About a week later, I find myself in front of my corporate computer in the middle of my workday.

This feels like... walking through waist-high sludge... I think to
myself as I click mindlessly, completing mundane tasks. An instant
message pops up and I groan, another person asking the same
question that was asked by a different person just hours prior.

Why is this feeling so hard? I ask as I see my guides, in my mind's
eye, looking at me with *the look.* It's the look that says, *You know
why this is so hard.* I sigh, and they are right.

I think back on a conversation that my boss and I had a week
prior. He had asked me, point blank: "Are you taking the VLO?"

VLO stands for *voluntary lay off.* Like many other companies
struggling during COVID, our company has gone through several
rounds of layoffs over the last several months, and we were preparing for the next round. Employees were being given the option to be laid off voluntarily so as to leave jobs available to those
who desired to stay at the company.

I chuckled at the time and shook my head, "No... as much as
I want to, I don't plan to leave anytime soon." My manager and I

have an incredible rapport, and I have always been transparent with him about my career moves and professional development goals. Our rapport is so good, in fact, that he knows all about my channeling abilities. At this particular point in time, I had actually channeled for him several times, and he knows about my *big work* in the world. He is incredibly accepting of me, and I'm grateful for that.

"Okay... Okay. That's good to know," he had replied, and we continued our conversation. That evening, however, my guides gave me different information.

I was rocking my son to sleep, stroking his hair as I sensed him drifting off. Suddenly, the letters "VLO" enter my awareness.

VLO…? I thought to myself, asking my guides for clarification.

Take the VLO, they had said simply, as if telling me what I should eat for breakfast.

I sighed deeply, feeling the truth in their guidance while simultaneously noticing my fear that was arising. *Okay… take the VLO,* I repeated back to them. *Okay.*

The following week or so felt quite precarious. I began signaling to my manager that I intended to take the VLO, and I wrestled with how to tell Troy. I imagined that he would be unsupportive and panicked to hear my decision, so I began to consider my options.

I could just tell him I was being laid off involuntarily…? In my mind's eye, my guides were shaking their heads at me. *Ugh, I know. It's just… this is so difficult!*

The VLO date was in October; however, there was the possibility of receiving an extension to December. I considered Troy's reaction again and decided to avoid the unnecessary conflict by asking for the December extension, which my manager was grateful to hear.

It is now several days after I had already signaled my intention to take the VLO to my leadership team. I breathe in deeply preparing to have the dreaded conversation with Troy.

"Hey, babe," I start, already feeling like a chickenshit. "Do you have a sec?"

We had just finished putting Finn down for bed, so it was now or never. He swivels in his computer chair to face me. "Sure."

"Well, I have something kind of tough to talk about." He sits up noticeably straighter. "It's about work."

"Okay," he says hesitantly, as if bracing himself.

"I want to take the voluntary layoff," I say much too quickly, and his reaction is fairly immediate.

"Wait, what? Really?" I sense his anxiety and fear creeping up quickly. I imagine putting up a bubble of protection around myself in an attempt to keep my own energy separate. I cannot spiral into his anxiety. I have to stand in my truth.

"Yeah," I continue, having a hard time looking him in the eye. "My consulting work is picking up, and I really think that now is the time, if ever, to make the leap."

"It's just such bad timing," he says. "I mean, with COVID and so many people losing their jobs…"

"I know," I cut him off. "But think about it… if ever there were a time to focus on diversity, equity, and inclusion work, it's now." I feel as though I am pleading at this point. But for what? Pleading for an escape from this job that depletes me in so many ways? Pleading to be seen by him? Understood?

He looks thoughtful, seeming to consider the argument. "I have to think about it."

"Okay," I say. I had expected that he would need some time to process. My own fears begin to surface, and I feel doubtful of his ability to be supportive of my decision. I push them away and turn to leave the room.

***

The next day, after putting Finn down for bedtime, Troy and I make our way to the family room and sit on the couch.

"So…," Troy starts, "I've thought about it. And…" I can sense his fear, and I think I know what's coming. He's not going to be okay with the VLO. I just know it. *Brace for impact,* I say silently to myself. "It still makes me worry, but I think you're right… now is the time. There is a wave of work that you might miss out on if you don't focus on your business."

I blink in utter disbelief, allowing my brain to catch up with what I just heard. "Wait, really? You're okay with this?"

"Well, I just think if you're going to leave and pursue this work, now is probably the right time… I'm not totally comfortable with it, but I think we can make it work…" His arms are crossed, and he is visibly uncomfortable. I know that this is really hard for him.

I jump to my feet. "Oh my gosh, really?! Babe! Thank you, thank you!" I run over to him and kiss him on the lips.

He pulls away and looks me in the eye. "But you're going to take the extension, right? You won't leave until December?"

"Right, I won't leave right away. We have a couple of months to get things in order, then a couple of months of severance."

"Okay. I guess we're doing this…" I can still hear the hesitancy in his voice, but in this moment, I'm just so grateful for his support. I hug him tightly.

Time to move forward, I hear my guides say.

BEING VS. DOING

Several days later, I open my car windows completely, allowing the fresh, woodsy air to enter my lungs fully. I exhale.

It is early September, and I am driving my car up a narrow gravel road toward the Whidbey Institute on Whidbey Island, which is about an hour outside of the city. This weekend, I am leading a retreat centering the healing of women of color in the Puget Sound. It is the second annual retreat I am leading with my small team of women of color healing practitioners. We have done this before, and it feels amazing to be sharing space with them once more, especially considering how difficult a year 2020 has been for all of us.

This year's retreat is especially challenging given the COVID-19 precautions we are required to adhere to. No groups larger than 10 people and social distancing at all times. Face masks 100% of the time when not in sleeping rooms. I sigh, pushing my anxieties aside for a moment, as I open my car door and walk toward the group gathered in front of the main hall.

I instantly see several familiar faces and a few new ones. I am giddy being in the presence of such brilliant, divine women. It feels as though no time at all has passed since our retreat a year ago. After saying hello to everyone, I begin to walk up the steps toward the entrance of the main hall.

I push the heavy, wooden doors open and am met with a rush of nostalgia. This is a healing space. This land, this building. I walk into the main meeting room and close my eyes for a moment, taking in the beautiful energy around me. I hear birds chirping outside as I peer up at the round window of the A-frame, sunlight streaming in playfully as tree branches sway in the wind, casting light shadows in the bright space. I look up to see the beautiful wooden beams that line the ceiling. I instantly feel grounded being in the space.

Large glass double doors line the right side of the large room. I push one of the doors open, making my way toward the cabin that will be home for the next several days. Once I find my cabin, I unlock the door with the pin I acquired moments earlier and push the door open. The cabin is one of the newer ones, but there is nothing flashy about it. Simple pine walls, floor to ceiling. Windows line the top of the walls, allowing sun to filter in lightly. I set my bag down on the floor and plop down onto the bed, which is small but surprisingly comfortable, cozy. I want to crawl under the thick comforter and fall asleep for a midday nap, but I know that's not an option. Retreat attendees have already begun to arrive, and I must ensure everything is ready for them.

I sigh. "See you later, friend," I say to the bed teasingly, and I see my guides smirk in my mind's eye.

***

The next six hours go by quickly. I can sense that the women here have already gotten so much out of our time together, and we have barely scratched the surface.

And although I am a master facilitator and never allow partici-
pants, and rarely even practitioners, to see me sweat, I am a ball
of anxiety already. The appointment schedule has already been
modified a number of times to accommodate attendees' shifting
requests and priorities for care. Most of the changes have worked
out organically; however, the changes still require communication with the practitioners. This retreat is already so much more
organized than last year, due to my diligence and preparation;
however, something always inevitably happens at these retreats
that I cannot plan for.

By the end of the second day, I find myself retreating to my cabin quickly, my energy completely drained. *What is going on?* I ask
myself. *Last year, I was so energized and inspired. I still love everything that is happening, all of the connections being made and the
community being built... but something is so different this time. I am
so tired. I am not getting energy from this.*

You're not a doer, I hear my guides say gently.

But... I contemplate that for a moment. *I am. I am a doer. Last
year, this was so much more energizing.*

*Last year, you were creating something. You were a visionary, cre-
ating. This year is very different.*

So, I continue, *if I'm not a doer, then what am I?*

You are a be-er, they reply simply. I chuckle.

A be-er? What does that even mean?

*Yes, you create. You DO in service of creating, of envisioning. And
then you pass that vision onto others to sustain. You are not meant
to sustain them, which is why you are so drained right now. You're
trying to be a doer, and you simply are not a doer.*

Well... then my whole life has been a sham, I say a bit jokingly.
*Doing is all I've ever known. It's all I've ever been valued for. Nobody
is valued for being.*

Well, then… perhaps it's time to change that.
And with that, they are gone.

17

A WRITER EMERGES

Several days later, I am back home and stepping outside to prepare for my call with my friend, Cait. She and I work at the same corporate job, and we both have decided to take the voluntary layoff. Cait recently gave birth to her first child and was on maternity leave when I reconnected with her several weeks ago.

I sit down on a patio chair on our deck and pick up a bundle of dried sage. I light the sage and begin to move the bundle up and down my body, guiding the smoke around me to clear my energy before my talk with Cait. As I continue my clearing ritual, I think back to the conversation I had with her a few weeks prior when I had brought her to this side of the veil.

We had been video-chatting, and I could sense that she was in full-on mom-mode, trying her best to listen to my words and carry on a conversation with me but completely distracted by her adorable baby boy.

"But how are *you* doing, Leilani? You're doing so much in your business—it's exciting!" she said.

"I'm really great, actually," I responded. "Remember how we talked about spirituality before you went on maternity leave?"

"Oh, yeah...," she said, rocking her son and trying to give him a pacifier to calm his squirming.

"Well, something big is happening, and I think you are supposed to be a part of it," I said. "Do you ever feel like things just aren't right? Like there is more here that we cannot see with our two eyes? Are you sensing any of this?"

"Oh, yeah...," she said, and I smiled, noting that she was completely distracted.

"Cait," I said gently, "I think you are meant for more than what you're seeing. And I think you know that, too."

She stopped and looked at me. I watched comprehension spread across her face. "Wait—what do you mean?"

"Well, let me ask you... how have you been feeling lately with everything going on? The racial unrest? COVID?"

She looks contemplative for a moment before responding. "Well... I think something is seriously wrong. But I also feel like I should be doing more... I *could be* doing more. I just don't know what that is."

I smiled as I heard a voice in my head say: *she's ready.*

"Cait, there's so much more to our existence than what you're seeing with your two eyes. But you have to say yes... to letting go of things as you know it. Are you ready to let go of things as you know it?"

"I... trust you. Yes," Cait responded, and I smiled. I took a deep breath and guided her through the veil.

In this present moment, I feel warm with affection as I set the sage down and begin to scroll through my phone contacts, find Cait's name, and hit 'call.'

"Leilani!" she greets me warmly. "Oh my gosh, how are you? I'm so curious."

"Hi Cait! It's so good to hear your voice!" I reply genuinely. Her joy is warm and infectious, and I instantly feel a sense of ease.

"Ahh… it's so good to talk to you. How was your retreat?! I want to hear all about it." I can hear the smile in her voice even though I cannot see her face.

"The retreat was *amazing*," I say. "I had a major realization while I was there—I'm not a doer. I never was!" I proceed to explain the retreat and how the realization came about when a thought flashes through my mind: my book, my writing. "And, something is moving through me now so I want to honor it and speak to it, if you don't mind."

"Of course! What is it?" I can hear the genuine excitement in her voice.

"Well, I have really been loving writing this book. Like, *really* loving it. It feels so right. And…," I trail off as an image enters my awareness. It's me, in front of a large window and my laptop, writing. Sheer, white curtains frame the window, moving gently as an ocean breeze enters the room. I inhale, suddenly smelling it in this present moment, the unmistakable scent of salt water mixed with sunlight and sand.

I peer out the window past my laptop and see Troy and Finn, their bare feet caked with sand. Finn is older, probably by about a year or two. They are running after the foamy water as it gently recedes back into the vast, blue ocean, then laughing hysterically as they run from the waves crashing towards them. Over and over again. I smile as I close my eyes and feel the warmth of the sun on my skin, the mix of joy, love, and laughter wafting in the air.

"I'm… a writer," I say to Cait, surprised at how natural it feels to say that. "I am supposed to write. That is my purpose. That's what I am meant to do."

"Wow!" she replies. "That's amazing that you know that with such clarity."

"I didn't… not until just now…," I say thoughtfully, still processing the vision I just had. "My guides just showed me something. I'm writing, but I'm not in this house. We are somewhere else, on the beach." A few other images move across my mind's eye. I'm writing at my dad's house in the Philippines as my son splashes in the pool with Troy and my dad. I'm writing in a hut in a dense rainforest, maybe Fiji, as Troy and Finn watch a movie on a couch made of bamboo with thin cushions. I'm writing in a flat in Paris as Troy and Finn say goodbye to leave for the day. "I'm traveling the world… with Troy and Finn… and my writing… it sustains us. It allows us to have a 'home base'—I think it's a beach house, which is where I have always wanted to live—and we travel the world, staying in places two, three months at a time… and I keep publishing books. I keep writing. It's enough for us to live the life…," I pause to consider my next thought, "…to live the life that Troy and I have always dreamed of."

"That… That's beautiful, Leilani…," Cait replies, and I can tell she is thinking about what I just said. "That's your future. It feels real when you describe it."

I bring a hand to my face and feel wetness. *Have I been crying this whole time?* "It just feels so beautiful, so perfect. Like, who gets to live a life like that? I'm so at peace… and I get to just…," I close my eyes, willing the word to come forward, "…*be.* I get to just *be,* Cait. Because I'm not a doer… and I get to just *be*… and it's enough. It's more than enough. It's what sustains my family. I provide for my family, and it doesn't feel like work. It feels like… life as art." I let out several sobs, unable to control how it feels to own my truth, my purpose. It is somehow overwhelming and comforting all at once. And these tears are healing tears, signaling that I have been afraid to own who I truly am—what I have been put on this Earth to do—for so long. Too long.

"And you deserve that, Leilani," Cait assures me. "Your gift is beautiful, and you deserve to live the life you have always dreamed of. You share so much of yourself, your gifts, with this world. You deserve this. You are so capable, friend."

18

SURRENDER TO RECEIVE

Argh.

I stare at my screen, finding myself more and more agitated as emails continue to pour in, reminding me every several minutes that my efforts and my energy are still very much in demand in my corporate role. I breathe deeply, bringing myself to the future for a moment, to that glorious date of December 4th when I can finally let go of what seems like shackles in this moment.

I chose this, I remind myself as I breathe deeply, nourishing my lungs with fresh breath. *I chose the December date. I could have left earlier, and I chose this…*

My heartbeat slows as I continue to remind myself of the choice that I made to stay several months longer before detaching from my corporate obligations. *I am empowered,* I remind myself. *I am powerful. I am a part of something bigger than myself.*

My heart slows to its resting pace as I begin to feel calm wash over me. Feeling victimized is my trauma response, and I have lived most of my life learning to find choice in everyday moments. Tough inter-actions with co-workers, previous managers… *I chose this life, this conventional existence… and I chose to stay several more months.*

As I feel myself return to a more balanced state, I click away at my keyboard to answer a few more emails before shutting down my corporate laptop and booting up my consulting laptop. I have about six minutes before I join Carla again for the second session of my akashic records training. Although my breathing and heart rate has slowed, I still find myself slightly agitated and worked up.

I brush it off as I make my way into the kitchen. I grab an artisan chocolate bar out of the cupboard and tear open the paper wrapper and foil encasing it. I quickly break off a few squares before popping them into my mouth. I savor the rich taste of the chocolate mixed with hints of sea salt as I pour myself a glass of water. Chocolate, and most other flavors, taste so much better lately, now that I am perfecting the art of being present.

As I make my way back into my office, a pang of anxiety hits my belly. Troy's voice begins to sound in my mind, reminding me of our conversation a couple of nights prior. The reality of my decision to leave my corporate role had continued to sink in for him, and he was airing out his fears with me once again.

"I just can't believe the same ways you do," he had said, an air of resistance and defensiveness in his voice. "I know you think you know how everything will turn out, but…"

"But seeing is believing for you," I said, finishing his sentence.

"Yes." He softened his gaze, less combative now. "I just want to make sure we are not putting our family at risk."

"I understand, you are worried…," I reflected back to him. "But it doesn't feel like a choice to me. I have been called forward. I have this purpose now. What would make you feel more in control? What do you want?"

He looked thoughtful for a moment. "I want to check in," he said, finally. "I want to check in next year, maybe July, to make sure this still makes sense. I want to make sure you are bringing in enough income to help with bills."

"That's a fair request," I had replied, and I saw relief wash over his face. "Let's check in mid-year, and we can evaluate what's working and what's not. If I'm not making enough, we will figure out what needs to shift."

In this present moment, I click on the virtual meeting link that Carla sent to me. As I wait for Carla to admit me into the meeting room, I become curious about the agitation that I have been consistently feeling today… the anxiety in my belly. I am jolted out of my thoughts when I see Carla's face suddenly smiling back at me.

"Hi, Carla," I say, trying to bring myself back to the present moment. "How are you?"

"Hi, Leilani!" She is more chipper than I am, and I begin to feel guilty for the energy I'm bringing into the space. "I'm doing well today… glad it's Friday! How are you?"

"I'm…," I hesitate, fighting the urge to share the typical, very American, avoidant *'I'm fine'* response. "I'm… not great. I have been agitated all day and now I'm just feeling kind of… icky. Disconnected from myself…" I take a deep breath and study her face as she considers her response.

After several moments, she says, "I see. What has you feeling this way? What is coming up for you?"

"I guess…," I start, unsure of the answer to her question, "…I suppose, I am feeling afraid. I'm sitting with this notion today that I am quitting my job and only have a couple of months to really figure shit out…" I fidget with the cord of my ear buds. "…And, I guess… what if I made a mistake? What if I just quit my job and the money doesn't actually come? What if I'm not actually provided for?" I feel my anxiety taking over, and I get the feeling that I am beginning to spin out. I take a long breath and continue. "I just… I want to know what this fear is about… and if there is anything I can do to release it."

"Well," Carla responds. "I was going to go through the manual a bit, then go into the records." She studies my face, my posture. "But if you'd like, we can start in the records and see what comes forward. What would you prefer?"

I contemplate my options for a moment. "Let's start in the records."

"Okay, sure. Want to go ahead and bring us in? Just talk me through your process."

I close my eyes and begin the grounding ritual, vocalizing my process to Carla. In my mind's eye, I see a cylinder of white and golden sparkling light appear, making its way from the heavens and finding my crown chakra, the top of my head. I breathe in as the light enters my body, slowly filling it beginning with my feet.

A few moments pass and I find myself in the bustling market. People are milling about, and I see Joan of Arc coming toward me. She is so happy to see me again and greets me with a hug. I look around, searching for the glow of a vendor's cart that signifies where I should go to receive the information I am seeking. I see a faint golden glow in the distance and take Joan of Arc's hand as we skip dramatically toward it, laughing at how silly we are. In no time, we are dancing and doing cartwheels toward the cart, laughing and falling all over ourselves joyfully.

As we approach the cart, I see someone familiar. It's my father, but he is much, much younger. I begin to explain what I am seeing to Carla as I see it in my mind's eye. My father is probably about twenty years old and in college; he is wearing a bright green, 70s-style polyester shirt and bell-bottom jeans. He has a full head of hair and a thick mustache. The man I am looking back at is the man he was before he got my mom pregnant in college with my older brother, before his plans were completely altered. I giggle as he smiles back at me, his smile spreading his thick, giant mustache across his face. There is a twinkle in his eye. *Playfulness. Hope.*

Hi Dad, I say with a smile. He smiles back. He doesn't have anything on his cart to offer me. Instead, he shows me an image of him and his brother playing with fireworks and laughing hysterically. They are causing mischief, which is mostly harmless but feels really risky to them both. My dad is having *fun* in this image. I am not sure I have ever seen my dad so… carefree. Light. The message begins to come through.

Remember to play. To be joyful. To rest. To have fun.

I take several moments to consider how seriously I have been treating my purpose, my soul's work. It is important work, there is no doubt about that. But can it also be important work that feels light? Fun? Carefree? Can I let go of some of the fear of completely screwing it up? Something that I have learned over the past several weeks is the enormous capacity we have, as humans and divine beings, to hold multiple seemingly conflicting realities. To hold paradox. I can be here for something very important, and I can also laugh and remember who I am—that I am Purity of Spirit, a name that was gifted to me by my coaching cohort several years earlier. I am joy embodied. Laughter. Levity. Divine beings are all of those things all at once. I can *choose* to be all of those things all at once.

I breathe a sigh of relief, and it feels like the first time I have fully exhaled in days. I thank my father for the message and hug him tightly. It is so nice to see him this way, so carefree, before he was bound by obligation and responsibility. I let him know that I will tell him, in his current human form, the message and gift he has just given me, and he smiles even wider, his eyes becoming two small slits under his thick bangs. *I love you, Dad…*

I turn toward Joan of Arc, and she is smiling back at me. As I continue to look into her eyes, I remember my intention for entering the records. *I'm ready… I want to let go of this fear… It's here,* I say to her, rubbing my belly. *It's in my gut, this anxiety.*

She nods, acknowledging the request. I continue to breathe as her hands enter my torso. She is feeling around, gathering what appear to be formless dark shadows between her hands as she begins to draw it out of my midsection. She brings the dark energy toward her for a moment before lifting her hands up and allowing the energy to float upward before it starts to dissolve and disappear. She enters my midsection a second time to clean up what remains; the tiny slivers of darkness that she gently gathers and releases in the same way, dissolving it into the ether.

I continue to breathe and thank her silently. When I look down at my midsection, I notice there is still some residual darkness. *Why is there still some fear left?*

It's not yours, she replies. *The fear that is left is not yours and, therefore, I cannot release it. You still have a lesson to learn regarding your boundaries. You are internalizing fear that does not belong to you.*

Troy. I'm internalizing his fear. Without knowing exactly how I am going to set the boundaries around his fear, I thank Joan of Arc for guiding me through the records before arriving back into my body. I open my eyes and see Carla smiling back at me on the computer screen.

"Great work," she says. "You're such a natural."

***

A few hours pass and I am answering emails, wrapping up my work day. My phone buzzes and I look down to see who is calling. Typically, I would not answer a call from a number I don't know, but something tells me to pick up.

"Hi, this is Leilani," I say into the phone, still focused on the email I am crafting.

"Hi, Leilani… it's Marion…"

I stop typing and perk up. Marion is a contact from one of my biggest consulting clients, and I am genuinely grateful to hear from her.

"Hi, Marion! It's so great to hear from you! How are you?" We spend a few minutes catching up, talking about our families, the pandemic, and the racial unrest.

"I'm curious to see if you have gotten the emails that I sent you? I haven't heard back from you...," she says, and I can hear the kindness and lack of judgment in her voice.

I consider her question. "Oh gosh! I'm sorry – I must have missed them! Did you send them to my business email?"

"I sent them to...," I hear mouse clicks in the background, and she rattles off my personal email address.

"Ah! I see. You sent it to my personal email, and I must have missed it! What can I help you with?"

She goes on to explain some work they want to send my way, reviewing their impact plan for biased language. After getting clear on the scope, I say yes and thank her for reaching out. I begin to feel excited about the work they are asking me to do as my mind drifts back to the akashic records session from earlier.

It was literally hours ago that she removed the fear, I think to myself. *And now I have new work. I was worried about money and the possibility of not providing enough income to sustain my family, and the moment I released the fear, I received an opportunity. I received abundance.*

You must surrender to receive, I hear a voice say. I feel something click into place as understanding dawns on me. That fear that I released during my akashic records training... it was in the way of the abundance that was already on its way to me. I think about that for several moments before responding.

It's so hard, though. It's hard with Troy. He's so worried about money, and rightfully so. This pandemic has wiped everything out. He's afraid. I feel myself beginning to spin out.

Fear is a choice, they respond. *If you take a moment to come up a level, to see things from a higher perspective, you will reconnect with your purpose here, your divinity. In your perfect state, money does not exist. So, to be afraid of something that doesn't exist physically and is spiritually meaningless is a complete waste of your precious energy here. But somehow, in this physical reality, this dimension, as a collective, you have put money above all else, even human life and suffering. Surrender… surrender to receive. Money is just energy. Allow it to flow toward you with ease.*

Okay, but how am I supposed to get Troy on board with that? I ask.

That is not a concern for today, they reply.

Well, that's a cop out, I say teasingly.

I sense them smile. *It does not negate the truth in the statement. You are capable. Time to move forward and embrace your path.*

Okay, I say and begin formulating a plan to address the new business on its way to me.

19

SPIRITUAL WARFARE

The following week, I find myself in front of my computer again on a video call with Carla for our akashic records session.

"Okay," Carla says, "Are you ready?"

"Yep! Let's do it," I say, closing my eyes as I prepare to enter the records. Today, I am practicing accessing my own records, and it's the last session of my first level of training with Carla. I had told her that I wanted clarity around how to understand what work I should be saying "yes" to in the coming months—as a "doer." I have seen that I will need to stay in this "doer" role for a bit while I work on my writing, but I have become so overwhelmed in all of the "doer-related" things I have said yes to. It's taken me away from precious time with my family and my writing. I have been taking on too much. I need guidance around how to be more discerning about what work is truly *for me* in this transition phase.

I begin grounding myself, envisioning shimmering, liquid white and golden light entering my crown chakra, the top of my head, and filling up my body, beginning with my legs which are cross-legged on my computer chair. Once my entire body is filled with the light, I imagine it extending beyond my skin and mixing with my teal aura to create a new, more brilliant color which gently swirls and pulsates around me. I continue to speak out loud to Carla about what I am seeing and thinking, but my voice and hers simply blend with this experience, surrounding me in this moment.

I see the marketplace of my akashic records begin to take form in my mind's eye. Amidst the typical crowd of people within my records, Joan of Arc sees me, waves, and greets me with a hug. She then proceeds to roll her eyes and gently scold me, asking me why I haven't been checking in and coming to visit. *We are here to help, you know,* she says. *We can give you the information you keep asking about!*

I know, I know, I reply, acknowledging that I have not been prioritizing entering the records, and she smiles, seeming satisfied that her message has landed.

Joan of Arc, Carla, and I continue to walk through the market, and I see a large bridge on the horizon. I begin to cross it and soon realize that I am in Rome, Italy, walking toward Vatican City. I see street vendors selling souvenirs at the end of the bridge, but as I walk toward the vendors, they seem to dissipate and fall away. I look around, trying to see where I am being drawn to go next.

As I look straight ahead, I notice a large structure—a dome— that is glowing bright and golden.

It's a church, I tell Carla, and I immediately feel a pit in my stomach. I stop dead in my tracks as Carla and Joan of Arc continue to walk forward and eventually turn to face me. Joan of Arc grabs my hand, encouraging me to keep walking.

I'm so resistant, I say to them both. *Churches… religion… there is a lot of trauma here for me. A lot of keeping myself small. I don't want to go.*

Both women stand there with me for a moment, and after what seems like several minutes, I begin walking again toward the glowing dome. *St. Peter's Basilica,* I say aloud as I remember the name of the church I'm walking toward. As I approach the entrance, I notice the doorway is glowing the same golden hue.

I take a few steps toward the entrance and notice I am alone. I look back over my shoulder and notice Joan of Arc and Carla both standing outside of the entrance, smiling warmly at me. *Wait… I have to do this alone? I don't want to be alone… it's too hard…,* I plead.

You have to do this alone, Joan of Arc says gently. *You can do this.*

I slowly take a few steps and look around. I remember this church from my days traveling around Italy almost a decade ago. I see the elaborate statues, the incredible architecture. I see the beauty, but I'm disconnected from it, distracted. *What am I doing here?*

Suddenly, as if on cue, I see a small figure at the front of the church. As I approach the person, I quickly realize who it is.

Lawrence? Is that you? He smiles up at me, and I am taken aback by his bright blue eyes and honey blond hair. I drop to my knees and embrace him tightly. He wraps his arms around my neck and hugs me back. Any anxiety I had about entering the church instantly melts away. I feel safe, seen… right there in his arms. After a few moments, I wipe away a tear and step back to face him.

Do you have information for me, little brother? I ask.

I'm here to help you! he says excitedly. *I am going to help you figure out what work to say 'yes' to.*

I hear Carla's voice echo behind me. She is still outside the entrance. *Is there some way, some method, that may help you call on him for support?*

As I begin to ask the question myself, I am shown an image in my mind's eye. It is a picture of me and Lawrence at the time that I lived with him. He is an infant and has a giant grin spread across his sweet face. I'm so young—about 19 years old—and I can sense the sadness in my eyes even though I am truly joyful in that moment, holding my sweet baby brother. That was my happy place. *He* was my happy place.

You want me to put your picture… on my desk? I ask, as the image forms in my mind's eye.

Yes! he says to me. *You will need a reminder to check in with me. I will be on your desk where you make most of your work decisions.*

I allow that information to sink in. *Okay,* I respond. *That's easy! I can do that. And it makes sense to me.*

Ate, he continues, which means 'big sister' in Filipino, *why haven't you been writing about being an angel?*

I contemplate the question for a moment. *I… want my writing to be accessible. I don't want it to be alienating, I guess. It just feels…* I breathe deeply and notice the emotion arising. *It feels scary. Risky. What if people don't connect with it?*

Again, I hear Carla's voice echo behind me. *Is there something there? Something that needs to be cleared? Released?*

I guess…, I begin as I consider her question. *It's a protection. It feels like a way I've kept myself safe. Maybe in another life. It's not serving me anymore, though.* As I say the words aloud, I see an oval-shaped bubble begin to take form around me, enveloping me. It's a shield of some sort. I reach my hand out to touch it, to see if it is permeable. I often put semi-permeable protections in place to preserve my energy and emotions, especially if I know I'm entering a difficult interaction with another person. This shield, however, is hard. Not only is it hard, but it is thick plastic, like bullet-proof resin. I know, instinctively, that whatever purpose this protection had served in other lives has expired. It is now only keeping me small and caged in my own fear. My fear of stepping into my whole light, my whole angel existence, my whole purpose here on Earth.

Suddenly, I hear angelic music and look toward the sound. The sound is a choir of angels, shimmering and dressed in all white with brilliant wings outstretched behind them.

Embrace your angel self, says Lawrence, and I notice he is already holding his little hands up to the shield, sparkling light radiating from his palms. I can see the shield dissolving under his hands. *You will need your angel community. Find them. Connect with them.*

As I watch him work, I feel the pull to help. *Do I need to…?* I raise my hands toward the hard shield. He shakes his head without even looking at me. *Okay, I'll just… receive… I guess.* Generally, I am the one helping others break out of their cages, so I feel really uncomfortable letting him work on mine alone.

Suddenly, I feel warmth behind me. Joan of Arc and Carla have both entered the church and now have their hands raised toward the shield as well. I can tell a bit of progress is being made to dissolve the shield under all of their hands, but it is slow. The entire choir of angels fly over to help, and I can't help but giggle to myself. It feels so silly to have so many beings focused on dissolving this protection, this fear. *This cage,* I think to myself, *it's kept me so small. It's kept me so small in my own… my own…*

Divinity, Ate, says Lawrence. *You've been keeping yourself small in your own divinity. But now, it's time. It's time to embrace your divinity fully. We are your community, and we are here to support you. We are supporting you because you will be supporting so many on Earth. You cannot do it alone—stop trying to. You're not meant to. This is your surrender.*

I look above us, at the front of the church and see a large orb of bright, golden light. *Source,* I say to myself, recognizing the energy immediately. The light begins to swirl around us and the others take a step back from me and the hardened shield. The light enters the structure, joining me and filling the space completely with its peaceful yet powerful energy. It continues to swirl inside the shell and begins to permeate it from the inside out, causing cracks to form and spread quickly across the entire structure. Suddenly, the structure bursts and tiny particles of the shield, like dust, begin to swirl around us before they dissipate and dissolve, following the golden energy as it moves further and further away, eventually out of sight.

I sigh, noticing that warm, golden energy is still pulsating around me. The protection is still in place, but it has no beginning and no end. I am simply… protected. Boundaries but no cage.

I look down at Lawrence, and he is holding a sword, his giant angel wings brilliantly glowing white behind him. He is the most divine, angelic warrior I have ever seen. I have always sensed that his mission after he passed away was important, but now I see… his mission is so much bigger than anything I could have imagined.

I'm going to help you, Ate, he says. *You're meant to bring angels on Earth along. You are meant to show them the way. You are an important part of this mission.*

I glance over to Joan of Arc, who is also yielding a sword and shield. *Spiritual warfare*, I think to myself.

It's time to step into your power, Ate. And we're here to help.

20

COMING OUT

I adjust my phone, which I had attached to my tripod, several times. *Argh – late again...* I say to myself. It is 3 minutes after the hour, and I am joining Josette's live social media event. We have been planning our live collaboration for weeks, and my excitement for the moment is overshadowed by my self-deprecating judgment for being late.

I breathe a sigh of relief as my video pops up. "There she is!" Josette says, smiling.

"Hi!" I say, feeling the joy and relief begin to flood my body. Josette has been such an incredible teacher and guide throughout the last couple of months, and it's amazing to share some airtime with her. *Wow, there are a lot of people on this live event!* I think to myself as I try to push my nervousness aside. This is the first time that I'm truly "coming out" as an etheric translator, a spiritual medium. We have advertised this live event the last several days and it appears to have reached quite a few people, several of whom neither of us know.

Josette and I talk about how we met, the events of the last several months, and our own personal journeys of evolution and growth into our highest purpose. The conversation happens naturally, and I find myself more and more relaxed as time passes.

About a half an hour in, it is time for us to provide live readings, guidance for those who have joined us today. Josette takes a back seat and, before I know it, I am the only one providing readings. I easily tap into their spiritual energy and convey messages from their guides. As each reading ends, I see comments roll in from those who receive readings. People are validating the information I conveyed. They are in awe of the accuracy, and many of them are crying.

This is incredible… I think to myself, feeling grateful for my ability and the support I'm receiving from the spiritual realm—not just my guides but those of every single person taking part in the live event. I see glimpses of our spirit teams in the etheric realm. *It's a party up there!* I observe as I see our guides mingling and getting to know one another. They are dancing together, laughing, and having so much fun. They are also holding space for difficult emotions and information. It's beautiful and exactly as I would imagine it to be when so many likeminded individuals share space in the ordinary reality.

Before I know it, our time together is complete, and Josette and I are signing off. I had told the community that joined us that I plan to do weekly live readings, something I decided on the spot, but it felt right.

I breathe a deep sigh, noticing that I am still floating from the live event. *That was so fun! And so meaningful…* I say to my guides, and I can see them nodding.

This is part of your big work. This is where you belong, stepping fully into your power, into your unique gifts, they reply.

Soon afterward, I notice a pit in my stomach. Usually, this means something is wrong. I breathe into the emotion, trying to pinpoint the message. Nothing.

I pick up my phone and text a few of my friends, those who are also tapped into the spiritual realm. "Have you noticed anything… is anything wrong? I feel like something bad is going to happen. It feels big, like maybe something in our country or globally…?"

My friends all reply with similar messages—they are not picking up on anything. I connect with Meesa, and she does a quick intuitive reading for me and leaves me a voice message.

"So… something is definitely coming, but it's not at the macro level," she begins. "This… this is something coming that has to do with you specifically. I get the sense that it is regarding a relationship. Something is going to fall, to crumble. It's about you."

I swallow hard, unsure of what to do next, as I continue to listen to her voice.

"This is going to be hard, sis. I… I just want you to know that I am here for you. Whatever happens, whatever this means… I am here. You have me. I love you." The recording ends, and I am in a bit of shock. I trust Meesa immensely. She is quite literally *always* right with her visions, and I know in my bones that she is right about this. I continue to reflect on her words as I begin Finn's bedtime routine.

As I am rocking him to sleep, I continue to seek answers from my guides. One message that comes through stops me in my tracks. It comes through clear as day: *Darkness is coming.*

What does that mean? My question is met with silence.

What… what do I do? I ask, begging for any kind of wisdom, any guidance to give me a hint as to what they mean.

Keep trusting yourself. Keep trusting your intuition. You will know what to do when it is time, they reply gently. *We are always with you. You are never alone.*

Okay… thank you. I'll be ready, I tell them as I gently lay my sleeping son in his bed. I give him a kiss on the forehead before I close the door and head to my own bed, feeling spent from the events of the day. I climb under the down comforter and let my head fall onto my pillow as I enter a shallow, dreamless sleep.

21

THE RECKONING

It is late evening the following day, and Troy has been out for several hours with friends from work. I glance down at my watch: 12:12 AM. I groan, thinking back on our conversation that we had before he left. *He said he would be home by 10! Where is he?*

I sigh, frustrated. This is not the first time he has been out and forgotten to check in. When he drinks with friends, he tends to lose track of time and letting me know where he is. I wouldn't be so agitated if I trusted him to make sound decisions in that state, but unfortunately, that has not always been the case.

I begin to worry, considering the poor decisions he's made in the past when he has been drinking and decide to text him: "Hey, where are you?" I check my social media for a few minutes to pass the time, waiting for a text back. When I receive nothing, I dial his number. After several rings, I get his voicemail and hang up. I glance down at my watch. 12:32 AM.

I begin to scroll through social media again, but I am so distracted by my frustration that I barely notice what is on the screen. After another 30 minutes, I send a message to one of his friends, asking if he is okay.

"Oh yeah! Troy's right here. I'll have him call you," his friend replies right away.

I dial Troy's number and he picks up. "Troy!" I start, and I can hear the anger in my own voice. His friends could probably hear it, too. I don't care. "Where are you? You said you'd be home at 10."

"We ended up going to Jennifer's house," he says. "All the guys are here, too."

"What?!" I reply, and I can feel my anger rising with each word. I don't feel jealous—I know Troy would never do anything like cheat on me. But I do feel left out of the loop. I can't help but think that most people would check in with their partners in this sort of circumstance. It feels incredibly disrespectful. I realize that he is still talking, and I find my voice once more. "I'm going to go." I hang up, still fuming.

"UGGGGGGGHHHHHHHH!" I let out a guttural noise, my disappointment and anger mixing to create an almost unrecognizable sound. I also feel sad, but it's buried deep below the anger. I cannot access it in this moment.

I take a few deep breaths and find the energy to pull myself up off of the couch and make my way toward the bathroom. I turn on the shower and wait for the steam to fill the space before I get in. I breathe it in, willing it to calm my anger and my nerves. "I feel like a different person…," I hear myself say.

As the hot water runs through my hair and down my torso, arms, and legs, I imagine the anger as dark spots of energy throughout my body. I concentrate on pushing the anger toward my skin, toward the surface touching the water. Then, I imagine the water absorbing the darkness and washing it away, down the drain. Down to the Earth, to be recycled and made anew.

This anger. It's something that I have spent way too much energy hanging onto. And it's not just anger toward Troy, although I have spent a good amount of time, especially postpartum, being angry and resentful toward him. Subconsciously blaming him for all of the ways that I feel I am lacking as a partner and a mother. It's anger toward every person, every circumstance in this earthly, human realm that has taken away from my spirit, my pure essence as a spiritual being.

As the water runs down my back, pulling the anger to the surface, I suddenly think of my mother.

I've been so let down over the years… Tears begin to cloud my vision, and I feel my consciousness being transported to a different time and place. I am 18 years old, and I have just graduated high school. It is summer, and we are living with my mom. This is not uncommon; we always spent summers with Mom ever since our parents got divorced about 10 years prior. But there was something very different about this summer in particular; we were living with my uncle and aunt. My mom had made it very clear to us that we were not to tell our dad about that.

I'm transported to another memory, this time even further back. I'm about 10 years old and my father is on the phone with my mom, completely livid.

"Why wouldn't you tell me, Zane?" he yells into the phone. "I had a right to know that this had happened!" He listens to her response. "Yes, I want to press charges!" Pause. "He's a bastard. He hurt her and you don't want to press charges? What the fuck…" Pause. "Fine, fine. Okay, fine! Okay, but he is not allowed to be near her. Nowhere near her, do you understand me? He's not to be in the same house, nothing. I mean it, Zane!" He hangs up the phone. He doesn't know I'm hiding around the corner, just listening. A family friend had been watching us after school earlier, and I asked a simple question that sparked this entire debacle.

"Auntie…," I had said. "What does 'molest' mean?"

She had been laughing and suddenly she got really serious. I swallowed, thinking I may be in trouble. "Why? Why are you asking this? Did something happen?"

"Oh, gosh… no… I just heard some people at school saying it."

"Jac, Kris… can you go play in your rooms?" My sisters ran off, dolls in hand. She looked at me sternly, and I felt a pit in my stomach. "Lani… listen to me. You're not in trouble. But I need you to tell me the truth."

"Auntie, really. I just overheard some kids at school saying it." A feeling of dread came over me. I could tell she wasn't satisfied with my response.

"Okay, honey. It's okay. But I'm going to call your dad, okay?"

"Wait, why? Am I in trouble?"

"No," she said, pushing hair off my face and behind my ear. "You're not in trouble, honey."

My dad must have left work immediately because he was home in a matter of minutes, talking to our family friend in the driveway. I watched from my bedroom, peeking through the blinds. His head dropped and his friend put her hand on his shoulder before getting in her car and driving away. I saw him take a deep breath and walk toward the house. I jumped away from the window and ran to my bed, holding a book, trying to seem inconspicuous. I heard a knock at the door.

"Lani, it's Dad. Can I come in?"

"Hi Dad, yeah," I replied. There are big gaps in my memory when it comes to the sexual abuse and interestingly, this is one of them. I remember my dad entering my room and I remember beginning to tell him everything. I remember the anger and grief on his face, and as an empath, I felt every single one of his emotions, including the guilt of not knowing and not being able to do anything about it. But I don't remember what I actually said. I just know it all came pouring out, like rushing water behind a dam that could no longer hold it. I remember him giving me a big hug and saying he was sorry that it happened. Then, I remember thinking he seemed so calm when he rose to call my mom, who had found out about the abuse a few years earlier. I didn't tell him this, but she had asked me to promise not to tell my dad. As a child, I had been the bearer and holder of so many secrets, my anger and pain kept loosely under lock and key, a burden that no child should ever have to bear.

Now, at the age of 18, I hear Auntie Kim asking my uncle and mom why my dad is so angry.

"Why would Ed be mad that we are here?" she asks repeatedly. "It doesn't make any sense to me."

My sisters are both upstairs already, playing video games on the N64. I am sitting at the top of the stairs again, listening. I have spent so much of my life listening and waiting for a grown-up to do the right thing, to defend me, to validate me. In this moment, I just want my mom to have my back, to tell the truth, and to help me feel as though his behavior and treatment toward me was inexcusable and disgusting. I should have known better.

"Derrick… did some stupid things… he was young and stupid," I hear my mom start.

"What does that mean?" Auntie Kim asks.

"He… touched Lani inappropriately. He did some things. He was 18…"

"What?!" Auntie Kim says. They continue talking and, somehow, it's resolved for them. I, on the other hand, stand up and walk into my bedroom and lie down on my bed with more burden, more pain, more anger.

I am a girl made of heavy boulders, boulders that make it difficult to walk this Earth lightly, easily. I see other girls, those who haven't had to navigate the same pain I have, and they seem so light, like they are made of summer breeze and sunshine. They laugh with their whole bodies and their hair and eyes sparkle. Oh, what I would give to be made of such things. Instead, I am made of heavy boulders of pain and forced silence. And my mother and aunt, two people I love deeply yet are unable to truly see me in this moment and my heavy boulders, unintentionally yet easily toss another heavy boulder on me; it instantly merges with the others. And suddenly, I'm in water. I'm drowning and the boulders are accelerating my fate.

I have this fantasy where I imagine another way that the conversation could have gone. In this fantasy, I would have felt... seen. Acknowledged. My pain would have been validated by someone, anyone. Somebody would have defended me, stood up for me. I would not have had to take on yet another boulder. Perhaps even a few boulders could have fallen away. Perhaps I would have not found myself in water. Perhaps I would have survived.

This is that fantasy, my historical rewrite:

"Why would Ed be mad that we are here?"

"Because this mother fucker," my mom would say, shoving a thumb in the direction of my uncle, a look of disgust crossing her face, "...is fucking stupid. He raped and molested my child, and, honestly, he probably really shouldn't be allowed in the vicinity of children. Like, ever. It's a wonder that he has gotten away with it for so long."

"What?!" Auntie Kim would say, disgusted. She would look over at Derrick. "How could you do that? I thought I knew who you were."

"I was only 18!" my uncle would yell, defending his actions.

"Are you fucking kidding me?" Auntie Kim would say. "You were the adult, Derrick! How could you? How can I ever trust you?" Then, Auntie Kim would stomp up the stairs. "Lani, let's go. Jac, Kris... you're all coming with me."

"Where are we going?" I would ask.

"Away from here. You don't have to be here with this disgusting excuse for a human. You deserve better. Someone should have protected you. And I'm going to do that now. I don't know where we are going, but we're not staying here. I am sorry so many people have let you down. You deserve so much better, and I'm sorry…"

Unfortunately, in this moment, my spiritual abilities fall short of actually being able to rewrite history. Instead, I'm here, in the present moment, with hot water falling on my face, which at this point, is turned up toward the showerhead, and I feel teardrops falling from my eyes, blending with the water and being carried away down the drain. This pain, it is the result of a lifetime of seeing all of the best in everyone, all of the ways that people are not living up to their divine potential, constantly expecting them to… and continually feeling disappointed and hurt when they do not. It hurts being the one who sees others' divinity and having to patiently wait for people to embody it, if at all.

Rarely does someone's inability to embrace their divine truth actually impact me in a meaningful way. Now I see, as my tears are carried away by the hot water of my extended shower, that Troy's inability to live into his wholeness is impacting me in big ways. I am tired of the drinking and how it gets in the way of our connection.

I turn off the shower and wrap a towel around me. I pull on a t-shirt and cozy pants and brush my teeth before lying down in bed. My mind is still racing, but I begin to breathe deeply, asking my spirit guides to calm my nerves and relax my thinking mind.

Then, I hear a car pull into the driveway. I hear a door slam and the car subsequently drive off. I get up to meet Troy at the door, my mind still spinning. I open the door and see him fumbling with his keys.

"Oh, hey…," he says.

"What the fuck, Troy?" I say, knowing that an argument will likely follow. I don't care. "You stay out way past the time you said you'd be home, you don't check in with me all night, then I find out you're at some woman's house?"

"Ugh… get the fuck out of my face…," he says, slurring his words and stumbling to get his shoes off. "Fuck you…"

"Oh, fuck me? Fuck you, Troy…," I spit back and I turn to walk away from him.

"Yeah, fuck you," he responds defiantly. "You're such a fucking bitch."

I stop dead in my tracks and turn toward him, feeling oddly steady considering the roiling rage that is simmering just below the surface. "What did you say to me?"

"I said you're such a fucking bitch! Go play with your Ouija board, you fucking bitch!" he replies angrily and throws a water pitcher across the room, which shatters as it hits the wall.

"I'm fucking out of here." I turn to leave the room, and I hear him call out after me.

"Yeah, fucking go. Just fucking leave already."

I pull on a sweatshirt and can hear Finn crying in bed. I walk down the hall and open the door to his room. "It's okay, honey…," I say, attempting to soothe him. I put his coat on and grab my phone and keys as I walk toward the front door.

"Wait, what are you doing? Don't take him…," Troy says as realization hits him.

"Well, I'm not leaving him here with you!" I step out of the front door, and Sampson bumbles after me. *I guess Sampson's coming, too.*

"You can't take him. I'm going to call the police," he threatens, and I laugh spitefully.

"Ha! Okay, call them. We'll see how that goes," I scoff, disgusted and enraged. I can see Troy capturing my license plate numbers before I back out of the driveway and speed off. I am surprisingly calm and steady. I don't cry or feel even the slightest bit emotionally flooded. I feel grounded, and I feel the strength of my spirit team in my bones. They show me an image of me in their arms.

There are so many of them underneath me, propelling me forward. I am not even touching the ground. They are carrying me to whatever is next, their wings moving swiftly, enveloping me in safety and warmth.

Thank you… I say to them silently as I drive into the night and away from the darkness.

22

CLARITY

I wake up to the sun filtering in through the blinds and sheer white curtains and the unmistakable sound of chickens clucking outside the guest bedroom window. I'm at my sister's house, in a small twin bed with my son sleeping curled up next to me. My temples are throbbing, and I rub them with my pointer and middle fingers on each hand, sighing. *What the hell happens now?* I ask my guides, looking up as if expecting to see a response on the ceiling.

Finn begins to stir awake beside me and quickly sits up. *How on Earth does he always have instant energy?* I think to myself, smiling.

"Hi, Mama!" he says sweetly, arms out and ready for an embrace.

"Hi, honey! Good morning!" I respond as I hug him tightly, trying my best to sound chipper and unfazed by the fact that we are in a completely new setting. I pick up my phone and turn it on. It's a few minutes before my first meeting. I sigh as I sit up, mentally preparing to begin my day.

I walk over to the small desk on the other side of the room and pull my laptop out of my computer bag. Working at my corporate job sounds like the absolute last thing in the world I want to do at this point in time, but I have too much to do to prepare for the final weeks in my role. I log into my computer and the virtual room of my first meeting as I multitask getting Finn changed, my line muted so they cannot hear the noise in the background.

Ugh, I really don't have to be in this meeting... I think as I begin to prepare breakfast for the two of us, passively listening in. I crack a few eggs into the hot frying pan.

"Hey, good morning," I hear my sister, Kris, say behind me, and I turn to face her. She looks surprisingly put together considering the ungodly hour. People have told us our whole lives that we look like twins, despite the fact that she is four years younger than me. Her long, dark hair is pulled up in a topknot and her tan face holds a slight smile, her dark eyes surprisingly alert.

"Oh, hey, sister," I say, trying to find the energy to smile but I cannot. My mind feels busy, and I am feeling stressed about the logistics of what's next. "Thanks again for talking with me last night, and I'm sorry for waking you up. Can I make you anything for breakfast?"

"No, it's okay," she says, and her smile fades momentarily, no doubt sensing my energy. "How are you feeling?"

I consider her question. "Stressed," I respond. "And... tired, I suppose. But like the deep kind of tired, not the kind of tired from only getting a few hours of sleep."

"Makes sense," she says, nodding. I faintly hear goodbyes in my earbuds as the meeting ends, and I pull the earbuds out of my ears. I use the spatula to move the cooked eggs from the frying pan to plates.

"I...," I start, trying to find the words as I focus my full attention on her. "I... don't know what happens now." I feel tears begin to sting my eyes.

"I know," she affirms. "It's hard, I know. You know I've been through the same feelings." I begin to think back to a couple of years ago, when she and her husband, Jonathan, had a brief separation. "You don't have to know what's next, not yet. You just get to settle in and take care of yourself and Finn. Knowing what's next is not a problem for today."

I inhale deeply, allowing her words to sink in. "Yes," I nod. "I know you're right. Thanks, sis."

"Love you, bish," she says teasingly and turns to walk toward her room.

***

Being at Kris's house is a welcome reprieve from the complications of my life and marriage. Finn and I spend several days connecting with Kris and her family, including his big cousin, Natalie. I get the sense that Natalie and Finn really need each other at this time, especially considering COVID-19 is still a valid threat in our community. *They both really miss people,* I think to myself as I watch them playing together. I smile, feeling as though some good may have come of all of this.

Over the next several days, I begin to browse available apartments online. The Seattle metro housing market is a nightmare, affecting all surrounding areas. Two-bedroom apartments begin around $1,500 in the suburbs, and those apartment prices reach astronomical heights in places like downtown Seattle, which I am not even considering at this point. I sigh as I feel anxiety creeping up in my gut. *How am I supposed to do this?* I think to myself, looking upward. *I know you all are carrying me, and I should just trust that everything will work out... but how is that even possible? How am I supposed to do this? I can barely afford my current expenses...*

Suddenly, a voice enters my awareness. *These are not problems for today. Find the apartment. Move forward. Keep moving forward.*

I breathe deeply, considering the guidance as I feel warmth in my feet, signaling that I am connected to the spiritual realm. *Okay. Okay. I'll keep moving.*

***

Several days later, I find myself just outside of the third apartment I have viewed in the past couple of days. Due to COVID-19 restrictions, I am alone viewing the apartment rather than having one of the apartment complex's employees with me as I view it. I have not gotten the sense that any space I have viewed just yet is *mine*. This time, I decide to be intentional about listening to my guides before I enter the apartment.

I put my earbuds in and pull up my music app. I pick one of my favorite playlists and put it on shuffle. *Okay…* I signal my guides. *If this space is mine, please show me a sign…*

I take a deep breath and push the front door open. Immediately, I sense a sweet energy as I take a look around. The kitchen looks nice, which has been feeling increasingly important to me. As I make my way further into the apartment, I notice the high vaulted ceilings. *Wow,* I think to myself. *I didn't expect to see that. Beautiful.* There is a large sliding glass door on the other side of the living room, which allows light to flood the space. It feels open and airy here, and I take a deep breath, savoring the beautiful energy of the space.

I hear a song begin to play in my earbuds and smile. The song is "Boy 1904" by Jónsi & Alex, and it's what I call my angel song. It is a song I discovered years ago, when I was just beginning to realize I have divine roots. It's a song that has brought me comfort in times of pain, and it continues to remind me of who I truly am. *This is it—this is the sign I was seeking.* I take a moment longer to view the rest of the apartment, but I know that my decision is already made. I go back to the apartment office and sign a 6-month lease.

23

QUESTIONING

"So… you're just going to move out?" Troy asks, a bit defensively. I am dropping Finn off with Troy for a few days, and he wants to talk. I don't.

"Yes, Troy. I have to do this," I reply, my eyes fixated on Finn as I breathe through the anxiety that is creeping up in my chest.

"And a 6-month lease? You couldn't sign a month-to-month lease?" His voice is slowly increasing in volume as he, undoubtedly, notes my lack of eye contact.

"No," I shake my head, eyes still on Finn. "They don't have month-to-month leases. Six months is the minimum. But… I will break the lease if I decide to move back in earlier. Nothing is off the table."

"And… the *only* way you'll move back in is if I'm sober?"

I sigh. *He knows the answer to this question,* I think to myself. "Yes, Troy. That's right. Alcohol has been such a toxic part of our relationship, our marriage. I will only move back in if you're sober."

His face hardens. "Well, I have been thinking a lot about this, and it seems like this is something you've wanted for a while. It's like you're using the alcohol as an excuse to leave. It just seems like there is something else, something you're not saying."

I feel my face get hot as I begin to breathe deeply. I feel so defensive when my integrity is questioned. *Source, be with me...* "Okay, sure. If we're being honest, Troy, I'm unhappy," I reply, my gaze now firmly fixed on him. "This is hard. I don't feel like you see me, and I've been saying that for years. I don't think you understand me. I don't think you even know *how* to support me emotionally. You are so resentful toward me. I can't do it anymore! And I told you when I walked in the door that I was having a shitty day. And this is how you choose to interact with me..." Tears form in my eyes.

"You're right, okay," he says. "Let's table it."

I give Finn a kiss and say, "Bye, baby. I'll see you later, okay?"

"Bye, Mama! Mwah!" he blows me a kiss as I stand up to leave.

I walk out the front door and get into my car. I turn the key and begin to back out of the driveway, heading toward my sister's house. As the house moves out of sight in my rearview mirror, I begin sobbing uncontrollably. I know in my head that I should pull over until I am able to get my emotions in check, but my heart won't allow it. I have to get further and further away from that house, the place where I have never felt completely safe to show up as my full self. From the person who has never quite accepted me as my full self.

As I roll to a stop at a light, I pop in my earbuds and pull out my phone to begin a voice message to my friend, Arham.

"Every move I make in the direction of my divinity, my wholeness," I say into my phone, "...every move is met with animosity, contention. It's like being my whole self is the worst thing in the world. Stepping into my divinity is some terrible outcome for him.

"And the worst part?" I continue. "The worst part is the impact... I'm questioning whether I'm a good mom. My son wasn't even upset that I was leaving. He just said... goodbye. He wasn't sad or anything. He was fine." I am still sobbing at this point and try to remember the guidance that I always give my coaching clients when they cry: *Tears are the physical body's manifestation of healing.*

"I'm just so deeply in my shame, friend. I hate this. I hate that he has this effect on me. When did I give up my power? When did I let go of it so easily?" I stop the recording and put my phone down, suddenly realizing that I am parked in front of Kris's house. I sigh and turn off the car. As I make my way up the driveway, I make the decision that I am going to tell her what happened. I make the decision to seek support. This is not something that comes naturally for me, but it is something that I'm learning to do increasingly as I step into the fullness of who I am.

I enter the house, make my way to her bedroom, and knock on the door.

"Come in!" I hear her say and I push the door open. She is playing video games and Jonathan is at his desk doing homework. They both look at me and, seeing the emotion on my face, turn their full attention to me.

"I'm just…," I say, choking back tears. "He's just…"

"What happened?" Kris says as she puts the controller down, and I can hear the underlying anger and protectiveness in her voice. I tell her what happened, and I can see the anger begin to spread to her face.

"I just can't believe that he is continuing to gaslight you! It's bullshit," she affirms me, and I breathe a sigh of relief.

"I'm not losing my mind then…," I say, mostly to myself.

"No! You're not. And it's awful that, after everything that's happened, he continues to gaslight you. This is not about you, it's about *him*."

My sobbing slows, and I begin to take deep breaths again. "You're right," I respond. "You're right. This isn't about me."

"No…," she says gently, her expression softening. "It's not."

I continue to breathe deeply and allow the calming effects of my breath to permeate my body. I notice my mind beginning to slow down, and I begin to think clearly.

"Thanks, sis. I love you," I say.

"I love you, too," she replies. "Have you considered going to an Al-Anon meeting?"

"Yeah, I think I will," I reply. "Thanks for the reminder."

24

SAFE LANDING

The next week was a bit of a blur. I rented a U-Haul, and Kris and I moved a few large items into my new apartment: my bed, a couch, TV, a desk, a cozy chair, a dining table. Otherwise, the space is empty and, surprisingly, I love the feel of it. A clean slate.

I am sitting in my comfy chair and pick up my phone to see that I have a video message from Grace. I smile as I watch her latest update.

Once her message ends, I begin recording my response and realize that Source has shown up to give her a message. I smile as I begin to translate the message, knowing that Grace will hear it soon. I then shift gears and begin talking about what has been surfacing for me. Suddenly, I am transported into my own mind and Grace then becomes a witness to my processing.

I am a child again, looking out the window of our military housing. I am eight years old, and my mom is walking away, holding a bag she packed minutes prior. I watch her walk away from us... walk away from me.

It turns out she doesn't go far. She ends up staying with another military family in the same housing complex. What feels the most painful is that I see her outside my window often, playing with this other couple's son. They seem happy, and I can almost feel my heart physically breaking. I am just witnessing. I could probably go play outside as well, but I'm paralyzed in my own pain, the pain of a child who feels abandoned by her own mother.

Source then brings me a level higher and suddenly, I am looking down on the entire situation. My mother… she's free. Free from the abusive patterns that she and my dad would get into. She is playing and happy. She chose herself.

I'm brought another level up. *She's an innocent,* a voice reminds me in my mind. I am reminded that my mom has always done the best she can, without fail. She did not abandon us; she chose *herself*. She chose freedom.

"She taught me that," I hear myself say out loud, my face wet with tears, as it dawns on me that I am still recording my video message to Grace. "I have been feeling so ashamed that I have abandoned my family, in the same way I felt as though my mom abandoned us. But… she didn't abandon us. She chose herself. And she showed me that it's okay to choose myself as well.

"I've been so afraid of *becoming* my mom," I continue. "I haven't stopped to acknowledge all of the ways that I'm proud to be like her, to have learned from her. She's so smart, Grace. And she taught me that it's okay to be psychic, to have spiritual gifts. She has always been an activist and instilled in me a spirit of…" I consider the phrasing. "She taught me to take no shit. Seriously. My mom has shown me that it's okay to prioritize myself and *take no shit.*"

For the first time in a long time, I feel proud. Proud of myself, but mostly proud of my mom for all of the ways that, through her imperfect parenting, she was still able to teach me the things I needed to learn from her, especially in this moment. She taught me the skills I needed to demand change in a marriage where I could not show up as my full self. She taught me that it is okay to walk away because, at the end of the day, I'm not walking away from Troy or Finn, I'm walking toward *myself*. Walking toward Source. I thank Grace for being on the other side of the screen and her willingness to consistently witness my process. I hit the button to stop recording.

I look over at Finn, who is playing with his toy dinosaurs, and I smile. Something that my therapist said to me recently comes into my awareness.

"Would you want Finn to marry someone who would not leave if they were unhappy?" she had said. "Would you want him to try to make it work if he wasn't happy? To keep fighting when he sensed things would not improve?"

At the time, tears were streaming down my face. "No, of course not," I had replied. "I want him to feel empowered to leave if he isn't able to show up as his full self, and I want him to choose someone who would do the same."

"You're giving him a gift," she said gently. "You're showing him that it's okay to choose yourself, and you and Troy are both showing him how to co-parent in a healthy way."

As I reflect on the conversation, I continue to feel proud; this time, I'm proud of myself.

25

THE ROLE OF SUFFERING

"Okay, honey! I love you! Have fun with Daddy and I'll see you in a few days," I say to Finn as I give him a kiss goodbye.

"Bye, Mama!" he responds, and Troy quickly whisks him away, no doubt doing everything he can to distract him from the meltdown that often ensues when he sees me leave the house. As if on cue, I slip out the front door just as I see them begin to wrestle in the playroom out of the corner of my eye.

I breathe a sigh of relief as I walk toward my car, not hearing any indication that he was upset at my leaving. I get in my car and take several deep, drawn out breaths before I turn the key and start my car.

This walking away from them… from my son… it feels so hard right now. I feel… I take a moment to consider how I am feeling in the moment. *I feel so sad.*

I sense my anxiety creep in, which is a familiar feeling for me when a difficult emotion is surfacing, when I'm trying to push another feeling down. *There is something here, along with this sadness. I need to honor this.*

A few minutes later, I find myself opening the front door to my apartment and setting my keys on the counter. The anxiety that had surfaced prior to and during my drive home has become more and more palpable, and I begin to rub my lower back, noticing a sharp pain there for the first time today. *I need to move my body.*

I roll out my yoga mat as I continue to notice the anxiety that is surfacing. I dim the lights and pour water into my essential oil diffuser, along with a few drops of lavender, bergamot, and sandalwood. I turn it on and breathe deeply as I allow the scents to permeate my spirit. I turn on a playlist called "Tibetan Healing Sounds," put on a chunky sweater, and make my way to the mat. The moment I find myself in the kneeling position, I begin to sob uncontrollably.

This is so hard. It is so difficult to walk away, I say to myself, seeking reassurance from my guides. I continue to cry, and I am met with an image in my mind's eye: they are surrounding me. I am in the kneeling position, my wings tight against my body, and they are all around me, hugging and comforting me. They don't say anything; they are just allowing me to *be*, to feel in this moment, exactly as I feel.

In the last few weeks since I left Troy, I have felt mostly upbeat and optimistic. Clear. Justified in my actions. But there have been a few moments of sitting deeply in my grief, in my deep, dark hole of despair. I've found that, in these moments, I need a couple of things.

The first thing I need is to allow myself to feel. To feel ALL of the feelings that arise without exception. To do everything in my power to release anything that is holding me back from feeling fully. In this moment, it is my physical body. It is aching and in pain and I know that it is holding onto something which is calling for release. As I move my body into different yin yoga poses, I begin to sob more loudly, giving my body and my spirit permission to release all of the grief that I have been holding at bay for the last couple of weeks.

The second thing I need is connection. My mind begins to shuffle through all of the people who I would normally call on for support. Kris? No, she's studying for an important exam. Grace? No, it's her kids' bedtime.

My sobs begin to get quieter as I feel the tension releasing in my back. At this point, I am breathing out of my mouth because the crying has completely blocked my sinuses. I look down at my watch. *Has it really been an hour that I have been crying on my yoga mat?*

I look up at the picture on my bookshelf. It's a family photo—me, Troy, and Finn when he was about six months old. Troy and I are both looking down at him and he is smiling back at us with a giant grin on his face. All the composure I had gained is suddenly gone, and I begin sobbing loudly again.

Why? Why is it that I have to let so much go in order to be my full self? I ask no one in particular. *Why do I have to grieve right now? It's not fair.*

I stand up and walk over to my phone. I am still racking my brain, thinking through who I can reach out to for support. *Anika,* I think suddenly and pull up our text exchange. Anika is someone I met recently through a mutual friend. She is also an Earth angel and a channel; although, she did not realize she was a channel until our first conversation. I had brought her across the veil about a month ago, right before Troy and I separated. And although Anika and I have never met in person, I know we are deeply connected energetically. Spiritually. We have traveled so many lives together. One as sisters. Another as best friends. I see an image of her in my mind's eye: long, dark braids framing a rich brown, beautiful face. Her smile sparkles and her brown eyes glow with a knowing that all is well and, if all is not well in this moment, all will be well soon. She is deeply connected to Source and, right now, I know I am being drawn to her for support.

As I look down at our text exchange, I am surprised to find that I have unheard voice messages from her. *That's strange,* I think to myself. *I wonder why my phone didn't show me a notification?*

I begin recording a voice message to send to her. "Hi friend, I just realized that I had unheard messages from you. I'm sorry I didn't realize that until now. I will listen to them shortly but, right now, I was hoping that you could send some prayers up for me. I am so deeply in my grief tonight and could really use some peace..." I proceed to tell her about my evening, how difficult it is feeling to constantly have to say goodbye to Finn, and how much I feel that I am giving up by living into my whole self. By the end of the message, I feel even more exhausted; however, I am so drawn to the unheard messages that she sent me days prior. I hit play and begin to listen.

My eyes well up with tears again as I hear her pure words and beautiful message—no doubt channeled specifically for me to hear in this very moment. The message was simply that she was receiving guidance that Source sees her obedience and that she will be protected and looked after. *This... what I've been struggling with... it isn't just about me,* I think to myself as realization hits me. Since this all started, I have only said 'yes' to the path that Source has set out for me. I have been so obedient. As soon as it was clear to me that Source was using me as an instrument, I dropped everything and followed the path.

I'm not choosing myself over everything and everyone else... I think as I continue to process the thought. *I'm choosing... Source. I'm choosing the path set out for me. I'm being obedient as I gain awareness.*

I breathe deeply as relief and comfort wash over me. In this moment, I begin to realize how singular I have gotten in my own experience. I have forgotten how connected I am to the big picture, how interconnected I am not only to Source's plan for me, but also to everyone and everything on Earth and beyond. *We are not meant to experience the human condition alone. We are all connected and interconnected. And when we forget this universal truth, we suffer. When we remember this truth, relief and healing is on the other side.*

And, I continue, *suffering is part of the human condition, as is caring for ourselves in our suffering. It's important. Awareness of our interconnectedness is part of the human condition. We are not meant to be stagnant and only experience peace. We have to allow for all of it in order to gain the lessons we set out to learn when we arrived here. When we chose to be here.*

I pause, allowing the depth of these thoughts to permeate my spirit. In this moment, I am sad and grieving. And I must allow myself to be sad and grieving, in order to learn the lessons I *chose* to learn in this lifetime.

26

MISSED OPPORTUNITIES

A few days later, Finn splashes as he flails his arms wildly during bath time. He is laughing, enjoying watching the bubbles swish back and forth under his power.

Suddenly, an image of an old friend enters my awareness. *Stacy*.

In my mind's eye, I see him clear as day. Sandy blonde hair, bright blue eyes, and a mischievous smirk that always made me think that he knew something I didn't. Light, pale skin. Tall. Rail thin. I smile as I think back on our time together as kids.

Stacy was my older brother Greg's best friend growing up, and he was practically a brother to all of us. He spent long days and nights at our house, especially during school breaks. He and my brother were inseparable, and he was the mastermind behind some of our most joyful memories, like newspaper wars with all of the neighborhood kids.

Stacy and my brother drifted apart over the years, and he fell into a deep depression during high school. He ended his own life when I was in 9th grade, and it devastated me and my entire family, but it hit Greg especially hard. He and my father got into a heated argument one night shortly after Stacy's death, which resulted in my father kicking him out of the house. After some time, I moved into his room.

I have always been able to sense when spirits are around, and soon after I moved into my brother's room, I sensed Stacy there. It started with the sinking feeling that someone was in the room with me. I could feel that it was Stacy's energy and also saw vivid images of him in my mind's eye, and then I actually heard his footsteps. He seemed confused; he was looking for my brother. And although I knew he wouldn't hurt me, I still felt afraid. I always felt afraid when this happened, when spirits entered my space.

"Stacy...," I had said aloud at the time, as I huddled underneath my blanket, eyes squeezed shut. "He's not here. He moved out. And you're scaring me. Please go away."

And he did. I didn't sense or hear him ever again.

In this present moment, watching my son splash around in his bath, I become curious about Stacy and ask my guides why I hadn't heard from him until now.

His spirit has not yet crossed over, they explained. *He still has unfinished business in the physical realm, and the way that your gifts work, you don't have as much access to spirits who have not yet crossed over.*

Oh, I replied, suddenly feeling sad. I didn't like that he wasn't at peace, that he was still wandering the Earth, yearning for completion. Resolution.

I concentrate now on Stacy's image. *I miss you, Stacy. Do you have a message for my brother?*

I furrow my brow as I listen intently, trying to make out the message. *Something about... Greg's work... creativity? He needs to be creative in his work?* I think to myself. I turn my attention to my guides and ask, *Why is this so difficult? Why am I having such a hard time deciphering the message?*

Again, it's how your particular gifts manifest. Since he hasn't crossed over yet, the message isn't as clear to you. It isn't as pure, they explain. *Interpreting his message will require stillness and concentration.*

I sigh as I look at my splashing kid. *So... in other words, this isn't happening right now.*

That's right, they reply.

A few moments later, I pull Finn out of the tub and wrap him in a cozy blue towel. He is belting out line after line of "The Wheels on the Bus" as I put a diaper on him and pull on black pajamas with green dinosaurs. After a few stories, a few more songs, and a kiss goodnight, I turn off his T-Rex lamp and close his door, the sound of ocean waves wafting from his sound machine as he closes his eyes and drifts off to sleep.

I walk to the kitchen and drink an entire glass of water before I make my way to my bed and crawl under the comforter. I breathe deeply and begin to imagine shimmering, golden liquid light pouring from the sky into the top of my head, my crown chakra. I picture the liquid slowly filling up my entire body, leaving no empty space. I imagine my cells dancing with the liquid, coming to life. By the time the liquid fills my entire body, I look like a shimmering, golden silhouette of myself. That is when I see Stacy come forward in my mind's eye.

Oh, Stacy, I say to him, giving him an energetic hug. *How are you? It's good to see you.*

I'm doing okay, he says, grinning. I remember that grin. I love that grin.

You said you wanted to get a message to my brother? I ask.

Yes, he replies. *The first message is about his work, what's next for him. He will need to center his creativity to truly bring his soul's work to this physical realm. He's an artist. He will need to lean into that in order to fulfill his highest purpose here.*

Okay, that makes sense, I reply as Stacy shows me images of my brother's drawings and the music he has written over the years.

And... Stacy continues. *He still blames himself. For my death.*

I swallow hard. *Yes, I could see that.*

It's time for him to let that go, Stacy says. *He has held onto that pain, that guilt, for too long. It's time to let go. It's time for him to forgive himself.*

Yes, I understand, I reply. *I'll be sure he gets the messages. Thanks, Stacy.*

I also have a message for you, Stacy adds.

For me? I say, a bit caught off guard. *What is it?*

I have always loved you, Lani. Ever since we were kids, I've loved you with my entire being.

Tears begin to sting my eyes as he proceeds to show me images that do not seem to make sense to me. They are images of us, connecting in our twenties, our thirties, and beyond. We are laughing and smiling. At one point, we are... together.

If I would have survived my depression, this would have been a possible path for you... for us, he continues as tears begin to fall from my closed eyes. The images are so vivid, so vibrant, and I feel every single emotion as I begin to make sense of this lost storyline that he is revealing to me. We stay in touch over the years, moving in and out of our own separate relationships, and it's clear that we never get the timing quite right early in life. But we stay close and check in often throughout the years.

Finally, well into our adult lives, we find our way to one another. Stacy finally confesses his love to me, something that, at this point, does not shock me, because I realize over the years that I love him, too. And we allow ourselves to be happy, together. We have both grown so much over the years, but he always knew me, always saw me. All of me.

I don't show you this to be cruel, he says gently. *I show you this to explain to you what you deserve. You deserve to be loved so deeply, accepted so fully, by someone who knows you—all of you. You don't have to make concessions. You don't have to settle. This… this is what you deserve.*

My face is hot and streaked with tears. I wipe them away.

I… I don't know what to say. This was beautiful and… I linger for a moment to allow the emotion to come forward. *Heart-breaking. My heart is broken.*

I love you, Lani. I always have and I always will, he says. And in my mind's eye, I see him hugging me. He kisses my forehead gently.

I love you too, Stacy, I reply and continue to hug him for several moments. Suddenly, I get an urge to support him, and I feel intuitively called to say something. *Can I… support you in transitioning?* He looks at me inquisitively, and I continue. *I think I can help you transition fully… to the divine realm.*

Really? he responds and takes a moment to consider my words. *Well, sure,* he says a bit hesitantly. Suddenly, determination crosses his face. *Yeah, okay. I would like to try.*

I let out an exhale, a sigh of relief. Suddenly, I see the veil take shape in front of us, the glassy waterfall suspended in air. He reaches his left hand forward and in realizing that he can move through it, begins to bring himself through. His right foot gets caught in the physical realm, and I notice his ancestors in the divine realm; their arms are extended and waiting to receive him. Stacy looks back at his right foot.

You can let go, I say, echoing back to him the words that he asked me to convey to my brother. *You can be at peace, my friend.*

I… I can't, he says softly. *I can't go yet.* I feel his overwhelming sadness for his family, his parents and brother whom he left behind. *I still have things to do here.*

I sigh, tears falling from my eyes as I grasp for acceptance of his decision. *Okay, I understand,* I reply gently, which is only partially true.

I love you, Lani, he says. *Be good, kid.*

And then he is gone.

27

RELEASING

I open my eyes and realize I have fallen into a deep sleep after communing with Stacy. I squint as I turn my gaze toward my window and notice the sun is streaming in brightly through the slits of the blinds. I peer at my watch: 9:09 AM. *Finn actually slept through the night… and let me sleep in!* I am amazed at the thought.

I stand up slowly and move toward his room. I smile, hearing his voice as he plays. I open the door, and he immediately sees me and brightens. "Mama!"

"Hi sweetheart!" I greet him and we hug. I change his diaper and dress him for the day. Over the course of the next half hour, we make our way to the car, and I drop him off with Troy.

I have an appointment with Meesa in Tacoma, which is about 30 minutes south. Typically, I would play music or an audiobook during my drive, but today is different. My spirit feels heavy, and I know it's because of the conversation I had with Stacy the evening prior. I find myself thinking about it the whole drive to Meesa, asking myself why I feel such overwhelming grief at his words.

The vision that he showed me was beautiful: a life that I am stretching my arms toward but is completely out of reach. *What does this mean? What am I supposed to do with this information? I'm so sad... heartbroken...*

I look up and find myself parked outside of Meesa's building. *Oh. That was fast.*

I pay for parking and make my way into her building and toward her office. I knock on her office door, and I hear her say, "Hi! Come in..."

I push the door open and, through my face mask, smell the healing scents of her office. Essential oils. Burning sage and palo santo. I breathe in deeply as I greet her. "Hi! It's so good to see you!"

We take a few minutes to say hello and check in before she starts with her questions. "How are you feeling? What's going on with you?"

I spend a few minutes telling her about my interaction with Stacy, and I update her on everything going on with Troy. I feel tears begin to form as I sigh deeply and look back at her, wondering what comes next.

"Let's take a look at this energetic tie you still have to your relationship as it was. It seems to be pulling you back and not allowing you to move forward, to whatever is next, whether that is with Troy or not. Something must shift but that cannot happen if you are still bound to this old energy." She looks down at my left hand. "Can you please take your rings off for a moment?"

"Oh," I say, as I glance down at my wedding and engagement rings. "Sure..." I slip the rings off and place them on the side table beside me. Suddenly, as if my body is separate from my own consciousness for a moment, I am surprised by a flood of grief, and I begin sobbing.

"This...," I say between sobs, "This feels so sad. I'm so sad."

Meesa sighs, and I can feel the energy she is already sending to my spirit. "I know, friend. Just breathe. Release."

I am still crying and feeling surprised by my outburst when Meesa places a small, aquamarine stone in my hand. "Hold this in your hand, over your heart, and place your other hand on your belly." She begins to recite what seems like a prayer, but the sounds are muffled as I focus on the energy emitting from the stone in my hand. I begin to see my ancestors in my mind's eye and recognize Apu, Tatang, and Granddaddy—all of my grandparents who have passed on. I see Lawrence, and he is holding Granddaddy's hand. They are surrounded by an aquamarine aura, and I feel my tears beginning to dry. My breath deepens and suddenly, I feel peaceful. *I am healing. I am releasing. Letting go.*

Moments later, Meesa guides me to her table, and I lie down as she begins to move her hands above me, checking my chakras. I am in the room with her, and I am also not. I feel myself surrounded by her guides as well as my own. The room is crowded, and I begin to see myself on the table from another perspective. I am witnessing. Witnessing my own healing.

After a long healing session on her table, Meesa invites me to stand up. She places my rings on a selenite slab, clearing the energy attached to them. She then places them in the palm of her hand and extends them out to me. "You can put them back on now."

"I... I don't want to," I respond. "It doesn't feel right."

She gazes at me gently and replies, "Of course." She slips the rings into a small plastic bag, secures it closed, and hands it to me. I give her a hug and say goodbye before heading out the door toward my car to leave, rings in hand.

ACCEPTANCE

It is Thanksgiving morning, and it has been two days since my appointment with Meesa. Finn has been with Troy the last couple of days as well, which has given me a lot of space to process my feelings around my interaction with Stacy as well as everything that surfaced as a result of my healing session.

I sit at my desk in front of my computer, holding my chai tea with both hands, savoring the warmth radiating from the mug. I close my eyes and breathe deeply, something I have done the last few times that I have sat down to write my book. I silently set an intention for the message to come through, that I may be a clear channel today for whatever appears, that I allow Source to move through me.

As I open my eyes, I glance quickly at my phone and see a notification. Grace has sent me a video message. I want to ignore the notification for now and allow myself to be present with my writing, but something is drawing me toward my phone. *Okay, I'm listening,* I say silently to Source as I pick it up and click on the notification.

"Hi friend!" she greets me warmly and proceeds to tell me about her morning.

She then picks up on a thread that I had started in the message prior. "I agree with you… I do think today is going to be difficult." I had mentioned that I was anxious about Thanksgiving with Troy since the last time I was there, it sapped my energy. Mostly, though, I am anxious about having to explain why I am no longer wearing my wedding ring.

"…and in terms of the ring," Grace continues, "I think you could take the time to explain it… or it could just sound like, 'yeah, I'm not wearing it anymore.'"

I sit up straighter as I allow that interaction to play out in my mind. There is no explanation, just a simple acknowledgment of *what is*. "Yeah, I'm not wearing it anymore." *Is that allowed?* I know the answer to that.

I stop Grace's message and begin to respond.

"Oh my gosh, friend… when you mentioned the possibility of just saying, 'oh yeah, I'm not wearing my ring anymore,' I asked myself… 'Is that allowed?!' Of course it's allowed! I don't have to explain myself…" I stop talking as I feel emotion rising in my throat and tears forming in my eyes. "I don't have to explain myself."

I allow the emotion to flow through me before continuing. "I've been feeling as though this is all my fault, that I am to blame for how everything is falling apart," I continue. "And… I've tried to shift blame to Troy so many times. I want to believe it's actually his fault, but at the end of the day, I know it's not. It's not anyone's fault. It just… *is*." I allow the realization to permeate my spirit. "This outcome… it just *is*."

I see an image in my mind's eye, undoubtedly sent by my guides. It's an image of the work I am meant to do here, my purpose. My writing is a huge part of it, but I have also recently begun to take steps toward starting my podcast, which is something I have been wanting to do for well over a year. My purpose is to get these divine messages out, and I'm a clear channel. I am part of a larger plan.

I continue to share with Grace, in a stream of consciousness form; however, I am completely present with my guides as they continue to give me information.

Another image enters my awareness, this time about 15 years from now. Finn is a teenager and leaving for college, and Troy and I are together, still married. We were able to reconcile during this current split. We were able to make it work. It was a difficult 15 years, but we are now at the point where we are ready to let go. It is amicable because we are both convinced that getting a divorce is the best thing for both of us. I also notice in this vision that in those 15 years, I end up sacrificing a lot of the *big work* I am meant to do, my Universe-led work, because I internalize so much of Troy's fear around money and stability. Without the physical separation, I cannot help but allow it to inform my journey and how I feel about myself and my gifts. I question myself and how *real* this all is. I slowly walk away from myself and from my divine calling. Once the relationship ends, I am finally able to truly focus on my big work again.

But, in this version of your future, you don't have the impact you are meant to, my guides say gently, and I know what they mean. I lose 15 years that I would have otherwise been able to focus on my work, and being in such an intense, high-stress marriage for so long slowly chips away at my sense of self and my spiritual self-efficacy. I don't have the impact I am meant to have because there is so much inner work and healing I have to do, so much emotional clean-up. Sure, I still have impact, but not the impact that I am meant to have. The impact that I *chose* to have when I signed up for this life.

The notion of free will enters my awareness again. *Your life is a collection of choices, and it defines your path. This is not a sad moment in time—it is a joyful one. You are saying "Yes" to your divine purpose, your big work. Troy will meet someone who loves and accepts him so deeply and provides him space to heal.*

I am sobbing at this point, as they show me the vision of his future relationship. She is calm and gentle when he gets angry, something I have always struggled to do. When Troy and I have fought in the past, we would trigger one another, and our fights would become explosive. His future partner sees him in his suffering. She supports him in the ways he needs to fully heal.

You cannot save others and you are certainly not meant to save him. He must heal himself. Remember: it is not your purpose to save everyone.

They begin to show me the few visions I had left of me and Troy. Slow dancing in the beach house, our future home base. Traveling the world as I write my books—Fiji, the Philippines, Paris.

They ask me, *Are you ready to let go? We can support you.*

I quietly answer aloud, "Okay."

One by one, my guides surround each image and put their hands out, willing the memories to dissipate and float away, up toward the ether.

"They... they're dissolving them, Grace," I hear myself say in between choked sobs. "They are dissolving the last few visions I had of me and Troy. They are saying it's okay to let go. They keep saying, 'Not for this lifetime. Not for this lifetime. You have to clear... you have to clear it all out for the explicit purpose of receiving.' It feels like torture, but I know it's healing... they are things I would normally feel over months and years... they do it so much more efficiently now because they are saying I can handle it. I know I can handle it... it just feels so sad." I continue to sob, and they show me a memory from earlier in the day. I had asked my guides for inspiration for my writing today. I begin to laugh through the tears and say, "They are laughing with me now. They are saying, 'You asked for inspiration... here you go!'" I continue to laugh through the pain and finally settle back into the moment, translating the final thoughts coming through.

"Sometimes, it hurts to expand. I'm hearing the words, 'growing pains.' I am witnessing my own healing. And you're witnessing my healing, too, friend," I say to Grace. "Thank you for being here with me. You're so important to my healing. I couldn't do any of this without you. We signed up for this, you know. We signed up to walk this life together.

"This season... it's changing," I continue, still channeling from my guides. "I still have more book to write. I asked my guides this morning if I should wrap it up now... if this is where the book ends, with my relationship ending, and now they are saying... 'No, you're still missing a season.' I better get to it. I love you, friend. Talk soon."

29

DEATH OF AN IDENTITY

It is December 4th, my last official day as a corporate employee, and most of the trees have lost all of their leaves. I sit at my desk in my small apartment, gazing out the window as I hit "Send" on my last email. I breathe in deeply and exhale before powering down my corporate computer for the last time.

Suddenly, the notion of death enters my awareness as I continue to feel mesmerized by the bare trees outside of my apartment window.

Death is only a beginning. That was the guidance that was provided to me earlier this year as I was just starting to understand my gifts as an etheric translator. I did not know exactly what it meant at the time, but as I contemplate the last few months, it is making more and more sense.

Source has made it clear to me that when we leave this human vessel, we don't simply go back to the Earth. Sure, our physical bodies return to dust; however, our spirits continue the journey.

In the same way that our spirits move on from this life, so does everything else. We, as humans, tend to grieve our endings. Ending of lives, relationships, jobs. However, what has been made abundantly clear to me at this point is that endings are necessary. We must clear for the explicit purpose of receiving. Grief is a natural way for us, as humans, to clear, but it is only one way to clear.

The trees, I think to myself. *Their identities, their appearances… they shed them every year and are born anew. Yet they do not grieve, and we, as humans, do not grieve their transformation. The butterfly transforms without grief. The bears hibernate each winter and are made anew each spring.*

This… I continue. *This is my hibernation. This is my transformation. I am being made anew.*

Yes, Source confirms. *You may feel sad about leaving certain identities and relationships behind; however, what is birthed on the other side of an ending is joy. Ease. Stepping into the fullness of your purpose without restriction and without effort. This is the next season. This is the new beginning that is required for you to step fully into your purpose. There is no anxiety or fear. Just arriving.*

***

Several hours later, I find myself standing on my balcony, holding a lighter and the notebook I used to take notes for my corporate role. I wasn't sure why, but it felt important to burn it, holding space and reverence for the ways that my corporate identity shaped me into who I am while also letting go of the ways it did not serve me or my divine emergence.

I begin tearing pages out of the notebook, noticing all of the different colored pens I used to scribble notes on the pages. I see drawings and doodles that I sketched while I listened in on meetings. There is richness here and all of it is important. All of it has mattered. It is all a part of me.

And, I hear my guides add, *it is time to release it.*

I nod, holding the stack of now loose-leaf pages in my left hand.

I set most of them down on the balcony and pick up a few pages, folding them so that they will be easier to burn. I have a large, metal bowl nearby.

I flick the lighter and see the small flame glow gently and hold it against the first set of papers. They catch fire easily, and I toss them into the metal bowl. I do this several times, and the stack of papers gets smaller and smaller as the burning flame grows larger and larger. Finally, all of the papers are ablaze, and I begin to notice different colors mixing with the smoke. Blues and purples and pinks, all swirling together in a brilliant dance.

All of the sudden, the smoke becomes so thick that I begin to cough. I cover my mouth and nose with my sleeve and open the sliding door to go back inside. I continue to watch the flame dancing wildly in the metal bowl. It takes several minutes for the flame to die down, and, eventually, all that is left are glowing red embers.

I grab a pitcher of water and bring it outside, pouring it on the remaining embers. I hear a crackling *hissss* as the last of the heat is extinguished. I smile triumphantly as I turn to enter back into my apartment.

30

SHAME IS BORN

"Yes! I'm so glad we are doing this… how lucky are we to work together like this and literally do whatever we want?!" I say excitedly to Cait as we wrap up our phone call.

"Oh my gosh, Leilani… I feel like I'm pinching myself every day. It is a dream come true!" she replies. "I'm going to keep benchmarking and finding ways to improve the website. More to come!"

"Yay! Thanks, friend. Love you!"

"Love you!" she replies and hangs up.

I exhale emphatically and slouch back in my computer chair as I reflect on the conversation. I just officially hired Cait as a contractor in my consulting business to organize our business processes and to help us get clear on who we are as a company and who we take on as clients. As we discussed an hourly rate, I felt as though the rate was communicated to me by my guides, and when I said it aloud to Cait, she agreed. At the time, it felt divinely guided; however, as I sit in my chair, familiar fear begins to creep in.

How on Earth am I going to afford this? I don't have the client base to be able to pay for her support. Am I being too optimistic? Am I going to let her, and everyone else, down? A wave of anxiety washes over me as I feel the divinity of our conversation leave my body. I start to hear old narratives in my mind, the shame that I have internalized from growing up with an immigrant father. I've inherited a deeply engrained scarcity mindset and it is quite unshakable at times like this.

My dad grew up in the Philippines, an impoverished country, with parents who did well by Filipino standards but not well enough to be anything but frugal. I have vivid memories of my dad saying *no* to things that I thought were basic needs, like new clothes when ours were worn out and tattered. When my dad did say *yes* to something, especially something that felt superfluous, I was always grateful but also a bit anxious. It was as though I had to pay extra attention to ensure I cared for it appropriately.

I am gently guided back in time to a memory of us as a family at an amusement park when I was in grade school. My parents were already divorced, so it was just me, my dad, and my siblings at the amusement park, and we were in one of the souvenir stores. I had fallen in love with this simple, sterling silver ring. The focal point of the ring was my favorite bunny cartoon character. I traced my fingers repeatedly over the little silver ears as I mustered the courage to ask my dad if I could have the $8 ring. It felt like such a luxury, but I had never felt so connected to a piece of jewelry before. I took a deep breath and asked my dad. He said *no* at first, and I pleaded. He finally looked at me and sighed, "Okay. Okay, sure. But you're not getting anything else today! That's it."

"Yes, yes! I understand. Thanks, Dad!" I said and gave him a big hug. I was thrilled. He actually said yes! And I got to have this ring that I loved instantly. It felt dreamy. My dad paid for the ring and handed it to me, and I quickly placed it on my finger and smiled down at it for several moments before looking for my siblings.

My sisters were trying on sweaters with their favorite cartoon characters on them. We all knew that our dad would not pay such a ridiculous price for a sweater, but I remember it always being so fun to try things on and pretend like they were ours. I grabbed an oversized sweater and made my way into a fitting room as well.

I locked the door behind me and took my shirt off. I began to pull the sweater over my head and noticed that my ring, and specifically the rabbit ears, were getting stuck in the sweater. I gasped, terrified that I might ruin the sweater and that my father would have to pay for it. I imagined the anger and disappointment in his face as I quickly took off the ring and hung it on one of the hooks. I examined the sweater carefully and sighed with relief as I noticed that nothing had been damaged.

I made my way out of the fitting room to show my sisters the sweater. "So cute, Ate!" they squealed. We chatted excitedly for a moment, imagining what it would be like to be able to own such a nice sweater, knowing in our hearts that there was no way we would ask our dad to pay for it.

I made my way back into the fitting room, removed the sweater and folded it neatly before pulling my own shirt back on. I looked around the store and didn't see my family. I panicked briefly before noticing my family was outside, waiting for me. I ran to catch up to them, and we made our way to the next ride.

When the ride was complete, I gasped as I remembered my ring, which I had left in the fitting room at the store. "Oh no!" I said, "I left my ring in the store! I need to go back and get it."

"What?! What do you mean?" my dad said.

"I took it off to try on a sweater and left it in the fitting room...," I said as I quickened my pace toward the store.

I arrived at the store and hurried into the fitting room, searching frantically for the ring. It wasn't hanging on the hook any longer, so I dropped to my hands and knees and searched the ground. Nothing. It was gone.

I came out of the store, tears welling in my eyes. My ring was gone, and I knew that I had to explain that to my dad, who never purchased anything excessive, ever. He was going to be furious.

As I walked out of the store, he could tell from the look on my face that the ring was gone. "Why did you even take the ring off? You don't have to take off rings to try on clothes!"

"It was getting caught on the sweater…," I said quietly, and for the first time, I noticed I was staring at the ground. "I… I'm sorry, Dad."

"See… this is why I don't buy things like this for you," he huffed angrily. "If you don't pay for it yourself, if you haven't earned it… you don't have any respect for it. You don't care enough to take care of it!"

Tears fell from my eyes, and I watched them fall to the concrete beneath me. I hadn't looked up to face him. I hated when I disappointed him. I constantly sought his approval, whether it was getting straight A's or ensuring my siblings and I had clean clothes and dinner on the table. Being a disappointment to my dad felt like agony. In that moment, I felt so ashamed.

Suddenly, my cell phone rings and my awareness snaps back to the present moment, and I am in my apartment. I look down at my phone. My sister, Kris, is calling. I pick up.

"Hey sis," I say, still feeling a bit jarred by the memory. "What's up?"

"Oh, nothing," she starts. "I just had a free moment and wanted to check on you. How are you doing?"

"Honestly, I'm in a bit of a weird space," I reply, and I tell her about the anxiety I am having about money. "I was deep in a thought about this time we went to an amusement park with Dad, and I lost a ring that he had bought me."

I continue to tell her the story, of which she has no recollection. I, on the other hand, remembered it with vivid detail. As I finish telling the story, describing my teardrops falling to the ground, she says simply, "Shame is born."

I consider her words for several moments before the gravity of it hits me hard. "Whew, sis," I say, still processing her words. "Yeah, you're right. That's when my shame around money was born."

"Yeah, I just see Dad as an immigrant, deeply in his own shame," she continues. "I see Dad's suffering and struggling and striving. Obviously, as a child you wouldn't have been able to do this, but imagine if, in that moment of his scolding you, you looked him in the eyes and said, 'Dad—you're okay. We're okay. You don't have to struggle so hard. You can rest.' He told me recently that he had been having nightmares that he died, and we still needed him. Your shame was born out of Dad's reckoning with his own shame, internalizing racist thoughts that he needed to work so hard and achieve so much so that *we* didn't have to struggle in the same ways *he* did."

I breathe in deeply as I digest her words, which hit me like a freight train. All of the high expectations he put on me, the good grades, the financially secure job—it was never about me. It was about his dreams for me, so that I wouldn't have to struggle in the same ways he did. Suddenly, a thought enters my awareness.

"But now…," I say, processing as I speak aloud, "Now, I see the contrast. When I told Dad I quit my corporate job, he listened. He didn't seem upset or disappointed or worried; just curious. He already knew about my ability to connect with the spiritual realm, so when I told him I planned to leave, he just asked what was next. I told him that I was being guided toward writing and focusing on my business." I search my memory for his words, "He asked if he could be a part of it. He was fully supportive, perhaps even proud."

"It's almost as if he's reached a turning point, like saying, 'We've done enough. Now, we get to work on our wildest dreams. We get to rest,'" my sister adds.

"Yes, that's the contrast," I continue. "Then and now. When shame tells us, 'You're not done working,' growth and acceptance says, 'Stop striving and rest.' I've spent so much of my life feeling victimized by Dad, when in fact, we were both simply victims of our own shame. In that moment, Dad was deeply reckoning with his own shame. I imagine it as a hurricane inside of him, creating destruction internally which, naturally, created destruction in its path… that's how *my* shame was born. That's how the cycle gets passed on for generations.

"And now," I continue, "Both of us are still reckoning with the shame, but it's calmer waters for both of us. Now, Dad has two kids…" I consider the thought before continuing, "No, four kids. All four of us are *resting*. I quit my corporate role that was slowly chipping away at my spirit to pursue more soul-centered work. You quit your job to find more meaningful work. Greg quit his job and moved to spend more time with his family and is accepting help from his in-laws. Jac is, and has been, living her dream as a dance instructor. Dad broke the cycle. We're all resting."

"I know you've been struggling with how to end your book," my sister says gently. "How *does* it end? After the reckoning, what is left?"

"Healing. Acceptance. And…" I seek quickly for the right word. "Thriving."

"Well, then," she replies. "I guess it's time for you to thrive."

"Yeah, I guess it is," I say, contemplatively. "It's time to write the last season of this story."

31

AWARENESS

I am a small child, about 3 months old. I am crying, so much crying. I am flailing my arms about when I notice my mother. She is in the room as well.

I cry louder. *Does she not hear me?* A whisper of a thought. A whisper of consciousness.

Louder and louder. Crying and crying.

What if… my consciousness drifts to my arms. I reach my little hands toward her. *Perhaps I can reach her, if only I try hard enough.*

It is not working.

I continue to cry, looking at her. *How can she not hear me? She has heard me before. I know it. I sense it. She can hear me.*

Suddenly, my consciousness shifts to my mother. Her back is to me, and she is facing the… light. She is facing the… *What is it called? Window? Yes, window.* She is looking out the window, but I can sense her. I can feel her… emotions. Her energy. Her yearning. Her grief.

She is… sad. Alone. Isolated. Unseen.

I am still crying, but now I am no longer crying for myself. I now cry for her. Her suffering is greater than mine in this moment.

I can help! A whisper of consciousness growing stronger and stronger. *I know I can. I know I can help. Let me help.*

I continue my futile efforts to reach for her. *Argh, these tiny arms. This useless body. So limited. So restricted.*

I cry and cry. Louder and louder.

Without looking at me, my mother turns and leaves the room.

32

REVISIONIST HISTORY

"Maybe… we have the power to go back and change our reality," Grace says. She and I have been discussing the fluidity of time and space for months now, and in this particular video message, something is clicking together for me.

My mind drifts to the possibility. *Revisionist history.* The term has been circling my thoughts for weeks now, so much so that I am convinced that my guides are trying to tell me something. There is a message for me here.

Their words, given to me very early on in my journey, fill my thoughts. *You are accessing the fluidity of time.*

If time is fluid, I ask, *then wouldn't I be able to change events from the past?*

An image enters my mind. I see my therapist sitting across from me. She is speaking to me. "Memory is not reliable," she is saying. "There are so many things that can get lost in the ways we recollect things. Our mind tends to fill in blanks. It's just not reliable."

I'm suddenly struck with a notion that takes my breath away. *What if we can change our story by accessing the fluidity of time?* I think back to the ways that I have modified my story through writing. Auntie Kim sticking up for me when she found out about the ways my uncle had been abusive. I consider the rewriting of my story regarding my shame around money, and how healing it was for me to go back in time and look my dad in the eyes and tell him that we are okay, and he can rest.

"Holy… shit…," I say out loud as the concept continues to form in my mind. My brain is working overtime, no doubt with the support of my guides and Source, to make instant connections in the moment. It happens so quickly that my breath begins to quicken. I pick up my phone to send a message to Josette. "I think I'm onto something here. We have the power to… revise our histories and to heal them… we do. I feel like that's what's happening in my book. Through telling my own story, I'm showing people that our individual traumas have played an important part in our story, and that we also have the power within ourselves to energetically shift… what has created our reality today. Reality is just perception. Reality is just a construct. It doesn't exist. All that exists is this present moment.

"And if we are able to acknowledge that truth, that nothing we see with our own two eyes exists outside of this present moment, then we have the ability to shift our past reality. We see this all the time in the future, right? People saying that everything is energy, that we have the ability to manifest our future reality and existence, that we can create abundance and allow it to flow to us through the power of our thoughts and internalizing our future as our current reality.

"All I'm saying is… why wouldn't we be able to also do the same with our past? Why couldn't we travel outside of this current moment in time to a past experience and allow that to be our current moment? Time is fluid; we should be able to do that. And… I only have power over myself in that moment. I cannot alter the ways that other people show up, I can only alter the way I show up. It's always a choice. People always have free will.

"If I were going to rewrite my history and go back to that moment where my aunt found out about my uncle's behavior, I wouldn't need saving. I would not need my aunt to take me and my sisters out of the house. I would save myself… and my sisters." I close my eyes and consider what that new narrative might look like.

I am at the top of the stairs, listening as they begin to talk about why my dad would be upset that we were living with my uncle. I come down the stairs, angry, and they all look at me, silently gawking at my audacity.

"Oh, please continue," I say, plopping down on a chair and crossing my arms defiantly.

"Well," my mom continues. "Derrick was young and stupid."

"Wrong," I say. "He was 18 years old—a legal adult. And he's not stupid; he's sadistic. And selfish. There is a huge difference."

"Who the hell do you think you are?" my uncle spits angrily.

"I'm just the child you molested and raped for years. Who the fuck do you think *you* are?" I glare at him as he shrinks back in his seat.

"When did this… how…," my aunt says, confused.

"It started when my dad was stationed at Fitzsimmons. My mom was working in the deli and Derrick was living with us and helping with *childcare—ha!*" I see the shame spread across his face and continue, "It didn't go straight to sexual abuse. It started with incredibly sadistic physical and emotional abuse. He made us drink his urine. When he was in a mood, he would make us squat and be on our tiptoes, shoving Dad's giant nursing books in our arms. The muscles in our feet and our legs would inevitably shake and if our feet went flat, he would hit us with a belt and sometimes with the belt buckle itself depending on how sadistic he was feeling."

At this point, Auntie Kim and my mom are both sobbing. I can't tell if they are sobbing because they are angry or because they are sad for me and my siblings. I continue anyway.

"He used to tell me to hurry up and finish my chores and to meet me in my parents' bedroom. He would order my siblings to stay in my brother's room and play, threatening them with harsh punishment if they did not. I remember one particular time I was sweeping the kitchen floor when he said it, and I moved as slowly as physically possible to complete the chore, without drawing attention to the fact that I was taking longer than usual. I did not cry because I knew that would have repercussions. It was the moment that I packed it all away, the importance of my own emotional well-being. That's when I learned how to *survive.*" My face is flushed and hot, and a tear rolls down my cheek. I turn to my uncle. "You stole so much from me. My childhood. My joy. My peace. And I'm not going to let you do that to anyone else I love."

I stand up and walk calmly up the stairs. "Pack your bags. We're leaving," I say to my sisters. Within 20 minutes, we are piled into my gray Dodge Neon and heading back to our Dad's house in Oklahoma.

My mind returns to the present moment, and I look down at my phone. I am still speaking to Josette. "Reality is just perception. Our current reality, what we see with our own two eyes, all it is… is a collection of thoughts. If we are able to go back in time, to our most traumatic events, and rewrite the story, we have the power to heal in this present moment, in our current reality. We have the power to heal ourselves; we have the power to heal one another; we have the power to heal as a collective. We have the power of our thoughts. All that suffering is… is a collection of memories. And if we are able to go back and rewrite those memories…," I take a moment to consider the implications, "Then… suffering is eradicated.

"The memory that is coming forward is my first ever memory. I am about three months old, and I'm crying. My mom is staring out the window, absorbed in her own suffering. I do eventually realize that her suffering is bigger than mine. I can feel her yearning, the feeling of being trapped in her life. She loves us, but she's trapped. I reach out to help, because I know I can. That's my purpose here: to relieve suffering. But she leaves the room instead, despite my crying.

"Revisionist history… I am three months old, and I'm crying. I notice my mother's suffering and begin to slow my breathing and stop crying. I begin to energetically… intuitively… telepathically… send her love. My mom looks over, and I shove my socked foot in my mouth, attempting to make her laugh. She chuckles. She tells me I'm silly and picks me up, giving me a gentle hug. She says: 'You're a good girl. So sweet. So special.' She takes a deep breath and says quietly: 'I'm sorry I can't always be more. I'm sorry I can't always be more.' And as she's saying these things, I see the suffering begin to leave her and fall toward the Earth. It's like the darkness is just a little bit lighter. It's not all gone, but it's starting to move toward the Earth. And I'm helping her… I am drawing the suffering out of her and inviting it to pass. And I'm not holding onto any of it because I'm a pure being at this point; I'm pure consciousness. I don't know how to hang onto anything, I don't know how to internalize, I don't know anything about boundaries or any of that. I'm pure consciousness and I'm just helping. And I can meditate on this and let this be the image that permeates my mind for the next several hours and let that be my reality.

"It's the same way we can alter our current existence and our future state. It's how we coach people around manifesting what they want and creating their reality. It's my saying, 'I'm a New York Times bestselling author' and creating cognitive dissonance in my mind. My mind says: 'No, you're not,' but my reality is already shifting. I'm already moving toward that direction. It works forwards and backwards. Time is truly fluid because we have the power of our thoughts, and our thoughts create our reality. We have the power to manifest a desired reality based on our mindset, speaking it into existence… why wouldn't we be able to do the *same thing* by going back in time, in service of healing and becoming more of who we are meant to be?

"Holy shit, Josette. This feels big. Tell me what you're thinking." I hit stop and send the message.

DOWN THE RABBIT HOLE

I am scouring the internet, looking up the term *revisionist history*.
I have very little context about what this term actually means, so I
want to understand it more fully. There is a specific resource that
I find on *contingentmagazine.org* that speaks to me immediately.
The article is called *What is Revisionist History?* and it is written by
an independent historian and freelance writer named Erin Bar-
tram:

> "Much of the time, [alluding to something as revisionist history]
> is meant as a criticism of the history being presented and the his-
> torians and organizations presenting. But what does it mean? And
> is it a problem?
>
> When used as a criticism in everyday conversation, 'revision-
> ist history' refers to conscious, intentional misstatements about
> things in the past, whether distant or recent. It can be used in the
> context of personal lives and relationships—the cause of an argu-
> ment, for instance—or in political and cultural discussions. At the
> time I was writing this, for instance, it was being used in Twitter
> conversations about Tom Brady, Obama's 2008 campaign strat-
> egy, and the Iran nuclear deal. Unlike saying someone is being

forgetful or getting confused about what happened, accusing them of practicing 'revisionist history' is accusing them of being a bad actor—a liar—by playing fast and loose with the past.

In most cases, accusing a historian of practicing revisionist history is accusing them of framing a historical figure, event, or narrative in a distorted and dishonest way in order to advance a particular social or political agenda. They're accused of minimizing or even ignoring evidence that would disprove their argument—or prove the argument of those who disagree with them. Those invested in the term and its use often claim they are defending history from people who are trying to warp it or use it as a weapon.

Often these complaints boil down to the belief that the historical interpretation that an individual knows, whether commonly-held or niche, is the correct one, which means other interpretations offered by historians are incorrect. Those historians, it follows, must be very bad at thinking, intentionally distorting the process and product of historical inquiry, or both.

But for some who use 'revisionist history' as a pejorative, the idea that history involves inquiry and interpretation is the problem itself. They'll argue that they're just looking at the evidence, not interpreting or "spinning" it like academic historians. History, for them, is just What Happened, its meaning easily accessed and understood by looking at a set of True and Complete Facts that has been assembled without human intervention.

If such a history existed, someone trying to change it in this way would be doing something dishonest. But I've never met a historian who thinks about history—either the process or the product—in this way. It's just not what we believe about the past or how and why we study it.

The problem, of course, is that the accusers in both of these situations are often doing exactly what they accuse historians of doing—ignoring evidence that complicates their preferred narrative or embracing a historical narrative that's clearly based on the interpretation of evidence but declaring that it's just What Happened—and therefore can't be questioned.

None of this matters, or even makes sense, unless we talk about why people accuse historians of practicing revisionist history. So I'd like to add one more thing to the definition I offered earlier. To accuse historians of practicing revisionist history is to accuse them of making conscious, intentional misstatements about things in the past, whether distant or recent, in order to make a point about how things are or should be in the present. The criticism is that historians are being "political" or "presentist," distorting our understanding of the past in order to distort our understanding of the present.

Consider the following situations where you often see accusations of revisionist history leveled against historians:

- *A historian making the argument that slavery was the cause of the U.S. Civil War—or rejecting the argument that there were black Confederates*
- *A textbook that emphasizes the role of women and nonwhite people in significant historical change*
- *A museum exhibit that reassesses the behaviors and beliefs of Richard Nixon or chooses to consider the effects of the nuclear bomb when exhibiting the Enola Gay*
- *A history department that requires majors to take courses covering a broad range of time periods and geographic regions*
- *A book that considers the competing intentions and goals of those who wrote, revised, and ratified the U.S. Constitution—and those excluded from the process*

It's not that historians are distorting the past to make a point about the present. The discomfort comes from the fact that historians are often disrupting or destroying connections people have already made between the past and the present, connections that may be based on no evidence at all, but that are an integral part of how they understand what the world is like, how it came to be that way, and what their place is in all of it.

Looking at the list above, it's easy to see how some people might feel that their present understanding—of their identity, of their community, of their nation—is threatened by new and unfamiliar historical arguments. If you're clinging to a particular narrative about the past because it's a small but important part of how you understand your place in the world, it can be easier to say this new narrative is distorted, and maliciously so, than to reconsider the old narrative. This is especially true when the new historical narrative, by considering more perspectives and new evidence and fresh angles, seems to be taking "your story" out of the center of the narrative, even just a little bit.

Now, here's the big reveal: historians do practice revisionist history, in a sense. They revise what they know and believe about the past. They do it all the time. It's kind of the whole point of the discipline. And it's a good thing. After all, would you rather historians never looked at new evidence? Or never used new tools and approaches to reconsider and reinterpret old evidence? Or never reevaluated the significance of old evidence in light of new evidence? Or never reconsidered questions that had been asked prior to the emergence of new evidence, tools, and approaches? Or never questioned things previous historians hadn't thought to question?

The questions and doubts that are part of accusations of "revisionist history" are very similar to the questions and doubts that historians express as part of our day-to-day work. What questions are worth asking? What evidence is necessary to answer those questions? Which perspectives should be considered? How and when does change happen, and who experiences it most acutely? These questions are part of how historians decide what to research *and how, and also part of how we analyze and assess each other's work, formally and informally.*

To revise means to look over something again; it's why students in the UK "revise" for exams. For historians not to revise in this spirit would be the height of arrogance, and yet there are times when we are too proud of our work, too defensive of our process, to listen to questions offered in good faith.

But when we're at our best, historians aren't afraid to revise— to look again—because we know that another look can only help, even if it muddles what we previously thought was clear. When done from a place of humility, rather than defensiveness, and its questions offered in good faith, revision is what drives historical inquiry. The danger is not in practicing revisionist history—it's in constructing individual and collective lives around historical frameworks too shaky to be looked at again."

I sit back in my chair, absorbing the information. I begin to process with my guides. *Revisionist history simply means taking another look at history with a fresh and, perhaps, very different, perspective. If memory is nothing but a collection of thoughts, if memory is not reliable, if traumatic events are creating more harm than good and getting in the way of our healing and our stepping into our wholeness... then who is to say we cannot go back and revise our individual memories?*

You're close, they reply. *You're not there yet. Keep seeking. Keep your eyes and ears open. It will come when you're ready.*

34

UNPACKING

It is the following day, and my sister and I are sitting on opposite ends of my couch. We are both drinking chai tea lattes out of large, ocean blue mugs, and laughing. I feel so grateful in the moment that she understands me so well. I have always felt so seen by her.

"I have a question for you, about my book," I say.

"Shoot," she replies and takes a sip from her mug.

"So, it is a little 'out there,' but bear with me," I start. Her facial expression remains unchanged. She's used to me being a little out there. I smile and begin to explain this notion of revisionist history that I am contemplating, and I ask: "I know it's not entirely new. I remember my therapist working with me to rewrite a trauma story of mine from a long time ago, so I know there is a variation of this that exists."

"Yes, it's called *narrative therapy*," she replies without hesitation. Sometimes, it's really handy having a mental health therapist in the family. "There is also *transcendental meditation*. That's more like hypnosis and it requires the therapist to rewrite the traumatic story."

"Right! I have heard of both of those modalities," I continue. "Narrative therapy is like accessing healing through the emotional body, almost like an emotional portal. Transcendental meditation is deeper, subconscious… like accessing it through the mental portal, or even the physical portal… What I'm describing," I stop to consider my next thought. "It's like actually moving through time, the spiritual portal, to heal traumatic events."

"Ahh…," my sister pauses, and I see her expression change as understanding hits her. "Holy shit. That's cool."

"I know!" I say, beaming. "It's different, right?"

"It is," she responds. "But it's not going to be accessible to everyone. It will probably require a long process. People won't be able to just access it right away. They need to get right with their spiritual body."

"I know," I say, scratching my head. "It feels tricky. Does that mean people will spend, like, weeks or months with me, training? Moving through the veil?"

"Well," she says. "I don't know that they have to stay with you for extended periods of time. But yes, I think they would have to dedicate a large portion of time and energy over several months to be able to learn how to heal themselves in that way." She goes on to tell me that it will be important to understand the two existing healing modalities. "I think it will be a blend of those and… spirituality."

"Yes, I agree." I think deeply about what she has shared. "I've been considering learning shamanism."

"Well, it sounds like you have some next steps," she says smiling.

35

WALKING AWAY

It's December 10th – Troy's birthday. I fidget with my face mask and, noticing I'm touching my face, immediately bring my hand to my side.

I am at the store deciding what type of cake to buy for the occasion. I had asked him days prior if it would be okay if I came over and brought dinner and a cake to celebrate together as a family, and he agreed. He seemed genuinely happy that I would take the time and energy to celebrate with him.

Later that evening, we had just finished eating dumplings and steamed veggies from our favorite dim sum restaurant. I am holding Finn in my arms as he picks up candles, one by one, and pushes them into the rich chocolate frosting, each one sinking in differently, each a little crooked. Imperfect yet bringing so much joy to his little spirit.

Troy comes up behind us with the candle lighter, the kind with the long neck, and Finn laughs excitedly as he lights each candle one at a time.

"Fire!" he says, pointing and giggling at the candles.

"Yes, that's right, honey!" I affirm him as he continues to giggle, gazing at the glowing candles.

Troy heads back to the table, waiting to receive his song and cake. I put Finn down and pick up the cake as we begin singing. I feel so joyful hearing Finn belt out the song, not even sure when or how he picked up the lyrics to it. *Gosh, he's growing up so fast! I can barely keep up,* I think to myself while still singing the song.

"Happy birthday, dear...," I sing.

"DADDDYYYYYYY!" Finns yells excitedly. "Happy *buuurfdayyy toooo youuuuuuu!*"

"Thanks, buddy! Can you help me blow them out?" Troy asks Finn. Before he can even finish the sentence, Finn is already blowing in a messy way, droplets of spit showering the cake. We all laugh boisterously.

"Do you want some cake, Finn?" I ask, grinning. I know the answer.

"Yes, *pweeeease*! *Burfday* cake!!" he responds, clapping.

I cut him a piece of cake—decadent chocolate with chocolate mousse filling and chocolate frosting. After he finishes his cake, we all sit together in the family room and watch a movie. It all feels so... normal. Typical.

Like old times, I think.

Troy stands up to start Finn's bath and I pick him up, making our way to the bathroom. I can feel him tense up a bit in my arms, a sure sign that his anxiety is starting to surface. He knows that it is getting to the end of the night, and I will be leaving soon.

I take off his clothes and place him in the bath before collecting my things, preparing to leave.

"Mama!" I hear him call for me, and I head back to the bathroom.

"Hi, honey! I'm right here," I say, peeking my head in. I see his eyes pleading, as if to say, *Please stay here, Mama. I need you.* I sigh gently, enter the bathroom, and kneel beside the bathtub. I ask Troy to hand me the cup full of water and ask Finn to tip his head back before I pour the water on his hair. I pick up the washcloth and put a bit of lavender soap on it before using it to wash his hair. I fill the cup with water again and pour it over his hair, rinsing the soap out of his beautiful brown locks. A little bit of water spills onto his face and he begins to fuss. Troy steps in with a towel, blotting his face dry.

"Thank you, Daddy!" he says and continues to play with his toys in the tub. Troy looks over at me.

"Thanks for the second present!" he says, playfully. He is referring to my taking over bath time. I laugh loudly and look over at him.

"You're welcome." I smile warmly. I begin to feel familiar dread creep up into my gut. It's the anxiety of knowing what's next: the leaving, the ominous threat of a meltdown.

After I finish Finn's bath, I grab a large, fluffy towel off of a hook and pick him up, wrapping him in a tight embrace. "Ahhh, Mama!" he says, joy washing over the both of us. I sit with him for a moment, patting his hair and body dry, and I look over at Troy, signaling that it's time for me to leave.

"Honey," I start, bracing myself for his impending panic. "Mama has to go now. Can you go with Daddy now?"

"No!" he replies loudly. "No Daddy!"

I sigh. "Okay, how about I throw you to Daddy?" I say as I stand up with him still in my arms. Troy assumes the position in the cozy rocking chair in Finn's room, arms outstretched and ready to receive him.

"1… 2…," I count as I swing his body toward Troy with each number, "3… Noooooooo!" I say playfully as I run off toward the hallway with Finn. "My baby, my baby! You can't have him!" Finn laughs hysterically as I run back toward Troy. "1… 2…"

We do several iterations of that before I finally "toss" him to Troy. Finn immediately starts wailing. "Noooooo… Mama!!! Mama!!!" he says repeatedly. I kiss him on the forehead and look him in the eyes.

"Baby, I love you. I'll see you in a couple of days, okay? I love you so much…," I assure him as I leave the room, closing the door behind me. I collect my things, unlock the door, and place my hand on the doorknob, still hearing Finn crying loudly. I feel paralyzed for a moment, unable to leave. Our dog, Sampson, is at my side, licking my free hand and wagging his tail. I look down at him, tears welling up in my eyes. He licks my hand again and I gently scratch behind his ear. *He's helping you remember that it's okay to leave,* my guides assure me.

Moments later, I can still hear Finn screaming for me when I am finally able to get the door open and step outside. The cold air has a bite to it, which feels fitting for the moment. I open my car door and toss my bag onto the passenger seat. I sit in the car for a moment, my hands gripping the wheel. A tear falls from my eye, then another and another. Before I know it, I'm sobbing and gripping the steering wheel tightly. *It never gets easier,* I say to my guides. *It never gets easier to leave them.*

I sense my guides sigh. *Yes, it's difficult, but it gets easier,* they say. *Just put one foot in front of the other. Start the car.* I put the key in the ignition, start the car, and begin to drive away, tears still streaming down my face.

JOURNEYING

I wake up the next morning to my phone alarm going off. "Ugh," I grunt as I hit the snooze button. *What the hell was I thinking scheduling an 8 AM dentist appointment?*

I barely doze back off when my alarm sounds again. "Okay, okay...," I say and roll to the edge of the bed before I swing my legs off and stand up. I reach my arms up and remember the bizarre and disturbing dream I just had. *I should tell Grace about it,* I think. She and I have been connecting around our dreams for years but much more so in the last few months. What I've realized about many of my dreams is that they hold messages from the etheric realm, and some messages seem to hold more importance than others. I get the feeling that this is one such dream, although I am unsure the meaning of it. I hurriedly change my clothes, wash my face, and brush my teeth before leaving my apartment and locking the door behind me. I walk to my car, unlock it, and plop myself in the driver's seat before placing my phone on the magnet holder. I pop in my ear buds and start the message before I begin driving.

"This dream... it was so vivid, so real." I proceed to explain the dream to her. I am sitting at a small table across the aisle from a small group of people, two men and a trans woman. The trans woman was a war vet who had lost her left leg, which was blown off in battle. "Left leg… representing the divine feminine," I say in the message as I connect links with the support of my guides. Her leg was gone, but through the magic of surgery and science, they were able to rebuild her leg. In the dream, her leg is exactly as it was before. She is whole again, renewed. Restored.

"But one of the guys she was with…," I continue. "One of them was upset because she was touching him, unknowingly. He was disgusted, appalled. I just watched, feeling so sad for her. But she took it in stride. She began joking with him, trying to make him smile, trying to make him laugh. Trying, trying, trying…," I say, and the connections continue to form. "She… is me. The guy is Troy. Once my leg was whole again, once I remembered who I truly am and remembered how it felt to feel *whole*… I was able to just show up with him, totally be myself. I try to be unfazed by his indifference, his disgust with me and who I've become, but…," I continue to remember the dream in pieces. "He… he left. He left me." I am still watching from the table across the aisle as I see the man stand up, still appearing angry and disgusted. The woman looks up at him, a look of helplessness and bewilderment. The other guy, also looking a bit helpless, followed him. The woman stands up and follows them, and the first guy tells her to go away. She reaches into her pockets and pulls out wads of money and throws the money at them, in a desperate attempt to get him to sit back down. The guy barely looks backs to scoff at her and continues walking out the door.

"The perspective I have in my dream, when I'm sitting at the other table… that's my higher self," I explain to Grace, the connections still being made by my guides. "The guy trailing behind Troy… that's his higher self. And I'm just sitting there, feeling sad and helpless. I don't know how to insert myself, which, I imagine is probably true for Troy's higher self as well.

"Then, I hear a scream. People are shouting to call an ambulance. I stand up and run over to find out what happened. The woman had cut off her left leg, the same one that was rebuilt. She cut off her divine feminine, Grace. She disconnected from her divinity. She knew that it was the reason for his leaving—that she was showing up fully, authentically. Whole. If she had stayed a man, broken in war, left leg gone... she would not have pushed him away. She's blaming herself." I sigh deeply as the weight of it all hits me.

"It's not my fault. Troy... he left me long before I physically left." My guides show me the numbing behavior, the drinking, the coping. The unwillingness to go to counseling early on or commit to it fully. He left emotionally, and spiritually, before I moved out.

"It's not his fault either," I am channeling the message now. "He is still wrestling with his own demons. They made it so that he could not accept me. He didn't know how. It's okay. It's no one's fault. But he did leave long before I did."

I pull over as tears cloud my view. "I knew I was blaming myself, but I didn't know to what extent until now. I have been completely blaming myself for how everything has turned out. But we both played a part, and neither of us are actually *at fault*. It's just... what *is*."

I am still crying as realization washes over me. "Revisionist history... that dream actually did happen, but in real life. And it could have, very easily, gone in that direction. I could have chosen to prioritize the relationship with Troy and cut off from my divinity.

"But right now, in my waking state, I can rewrite the story. It would look like this: my higher self walks over to the table after the two men have already left. I am devastated and alone. My higher self takes my hand and walks me outside. The sun is bright overhead amidst sparse clouds, a gentle breeze cooling the heat of emotion on my face. I close my eyes and breathe in the fresh air, suddenly realizing that we are in the middle of the mountains. In front of us is a gorgeous meadow of blue, purple, and yellow wild-flowers and just beyond the meadow is a large, crystal-clear lake, unmoving and still. In the distance, I see snow-capped mountains. I am surrounded by beauty and spiritual energy. My higher self sits cross-legged in the center of the meadow and invites me to place my head in her lap. I oblige and immediately begin crying as she strokes my hair.

"'All I did was be myself, stand in my wholeness,' I tell my higher self. *'And now... now, I'm alone.'*

"'I know it feels that way...' she replies. *'But you're not alone. I'm here, and the whole spiritual realm is with you. You're not alone; you never were.'"* It's as though my higher self is reminding me that he left, and I can't do anything about that. I'm not cutting off my leg. I'm not cutting off from my divinity. And last night, after I left Troy's with Finn crying out for me, I felt so alone—not spiritually, but physically. Now she's just listening to me crying and telling me, *'I know. I know it's sad when people leave. But you did everything you could. You even threw money at him!'"*

I laugh as I consider that. I truly did do that when I asked him to dream with me about traveling the world together when I'm a famous author. I was trying to speak to him in the language I thought he would understand: financial stability and security.

"Thank you for listening, friend. You're so important to me." I say goodbye and end the message and begin driving again toward my dentist's office.

***

I am exhausted by the time I return home. I can sense my guides beckoning me toward bed. I easily oblige and fall into a short yet deep sleep.

When I wake about 45 minutes later, I am still thinking about the fact that Troy left the relationship spiritually, emotionally, and mentally months ago, if not years ago. *And I am left with the tough responsibility of seeing that… and having to make the choice about whether or not to align the physical reality with the emotional and spiritual reality,* I think to myself. *I feel like that has always been my burden, my plight. I see beyond the physical, the mess behind the curtain. And it's up to me to pull the curtain back and fix the mess.*

I'm like a chiropractor, making physical adjustments, fixing things out of alignment.

No, my guides say. *You are not the chiropractor. Source is the chiropractor. This isn't your task.*

I stop to breathe in that truth. *Okay, so if I'm not the chiropractor, then what is my role?* Suddenly, I see myself bring a patient to a chiropractor's office, watch the adjustment occur, witness it, then leave through the front door and get back into my car. *I'm the Uber driver?* I ask, laughing.

Yes, in a way. You're the vehicle. You bring people to Truth. But it isn't up to you to save humanity.

Ahhhh… I respond. *That feels so much easier. Less burdensome.*

It may feel like it at times, they continue. *But you must bring yourself up a level in your perspective. When you are stuck in your human perspective, your ego… you will always over-function. You must give it over to Source. They will take every burden away. This isn't about you; this is about your purpose here. Focus on your purpose. Focus on the message. Leave the rest.*

***

Later that evening, I am lying down on the couch when I notice a channeled message beginning to move through me. I pick up my phone to record my thoughts via a voice memo.

The decisions that we make in this life inform what we do next. My guides are showing me the akashic records closing up at the end of our life, showing us all of our decision points… all the decisions we make in this life, kind of a housekeeping of the record of this life. I see myself as my higher self communing with Source and saying: "Okay, what's next? What do you see for me, what do I want for myself, and what makes the most sense for my next life?"

I see a meeting with my guides…they're like coaches, asking me what lessons still need to be learned. They're wanting to show me the process. There is a reuniting with ancestors and other soul connections when we transition to the in-between.

There is a closing of sorts… of our most recent life. It's so ritualistic, the spiritual realm. Debriefing the last life. Making sure everything is 'clean.'

Then it's 'being' for a while. Resting.

Soon afterward, there is a round table discussion. It's really expansive. It's not just about my life or even just my soul's journey. It takes into account the state of the world of the dimension I'm going into. And while this analysis is taking place, I'm able to pop into other dimensions to see where else my soul is learning. It's all so expansive. It's fascinating how much information we can hold in the spiritual realm versus what our human brains can hold and process. Source always shows up to everyone's round table, our soul discussions. The archangels don't show up for everyone, they mostly show up for the leaders. I don't choose my path alone. So, the fact that we try to do our work alone in this realm makes absolutely no sense. It doesn't work, regardless of how hard we try to make it work or try to convince ourselves that we have to do it alone… that we are alone.

When it's time to choose our next life, all of them convene with our higher selves and they say: 'Here's what's at stake, here's a mission, here's a mission, here's a mission, what lessons are you trying to learn, to take away, what does the physical realm require right now? What does that particular dimension require right now? These are the energies that are required, here are the gifts that are required, etc.'

And it's not a long meeting, either; rather, it's closer to an instantaneous download. Here's all that information, and I can hold it all, because I'm expansive. I hold it all like a giant bowl above my head, and I just evaluate it, and I'm very analytical on a spiritual level. I make connections very quickly; they are showing it to me like synapses firing. And I say, 'Okay, that's the one.' And I point to the path in the giant bowl above my head. 'This is who I'm going to be, this is the life I'm going to enter into.' And my guides say: 'Okay, did you think about this, did you consider that?' And I say, 'Yes, this is it.' And then I take my sword and my shield out, get on my horse, and I ride into battle because I'm a fucking warrior. I don't look weathered, though. I just look wise and knowing.

But I'm really curious… why do I continue to choose to go into battle? That's a question I would like to pose to my guides and my higher self. Because it doesn't feel like a proving, it doesn't feel karmic, like I'm trying to make up for anything I've done in one of these lives I've lived.

I'm hearing: 'It's required. Some of us need to go into battle. And you just always say yes.' I'm a keeper of humanity. Protector. Gatekeeper of Truth. And I get into my deepest, lowest places when I understand I can't protect everyone, I can't save everyone. My motives are very altruistic. Source has this deep love of humanity, and I'm obedient. I just say, 'What needs to be done? Where does protection need to happen? Where does duty need to happen? Where does valor need to happen?' It's not even a question.

And when people ask me that same question in the higher realm, when they ask: 'What is it that makes you keep saying yes to duty, to valor?' I say that I don't want to say 'no.' 'No' feels harder. 'Yes' is living in ease. It's harder for me to say 'no' than to say 'yes' to valor, to being a protector, warrior. It's me living in ease. I was made this way. It's how Source created me.

And Source smiles down on me a lot. They are always playful with me because they know how serious I can get, because it's life and death. And Source says, 'Yeah, I know it's life and death. I created it. But what is life and death without play? What is life and death without joy? What is life and death without levity? What is life and death without connection? Without pleasure?'

This is the new season. This is just the preface. We're all being prepared. It's time to step out. At the breaking of the dawn. At the first of the year. It's time to step out. I'm being led. I'm being guided. I'm being shown the path. 'Just walk the path,' my guides are saying. 'Do it with ease. Always with ease. Choose ease.'

There is no try. There is no try. There is no try.

Just ease. When I'm living in ease, that's when they're carrying me. That's when I'll have the most impact. That's when I'll be the most efficient.

They need me. They need me to step out. This mission was handed to me with the force of a thousand suns. It's bigger than me. It's bigger than my human body. It's bigger than even my spiritual body. I'm chosen. I'm protected. I'm seen. I'm known. They're saying, 'Never cut off from your divinity. Never sacrifice your peace. Never sacrifice your ease. Just attract. Attract abundance. Money is a tool. Money will flow. Stop worrying about money.'

'You have been chosen. You are going to be one of the leaders of the free world. You are one of the leaders of the revolution.'

AWAKE

I am jolted awake by loud banging. It sounds as though it's coming from Finn's room.

Is he awake? I think to myself. I peer at the clock. It's just after 3 AM.

I listen intently again, waiting to see if I hear anything. Silence.

As I drift off to sleep, I hear another loud bang. This time, it sounds as though it's coming from my closet. *What the hell…?* I listen intently and once again, hear nothing. I look at my clock. 3:33.

What is happening? I ask my guides.

The veil is thin. You're in between dimensions, they reply simply.

I drift back to sleep, still struggling to process what they just shared with me.

UNDERSTANDING

Where am I?

I look down at my hands. Pudgy and pale. *These are not my hands...*

I lift my head and look around. *I know this place... I recognize this place. Am I...?*

I am in a doorway. I see a kitchen. It's messy. Food piled on the counters. I see my sister, Kris. She's... younger. Much younger. Suddenly, awareness dawns on me. *Mom's old house. I'm in Florida.* I continue to look around. *Steven, my sister's ex-boyfriend. Oh my god... no...*

I walk clumsily and awkwardly to the living room which is just on the other side of the kitchen. My baby cousins. Much, much younger. I look down at my hands again.

Lawrence. I am Lawrence. What are you showing me, little brother?

Ate, he responds. *Be here now.*

I hear his words and begin to relax. *I am not in control here,* I realize, as awareness continues to dawn on me. *I am only observing. I can't change anything.* I want to cry, but it would take me out of the present. I am only awareness, only observing this moment. *It's important.*

Be here now, my brother repeats gently. I take a deep breath and allow myself to be guided, to be shown.

My baby cousins are watching a movie and playing, wrestling with one another. Laughing and hitting each other and being as siblings should be, as children should be. *They are so innocent.* I suddenly become aware of how much blame I was subconsciously placing on these little children, these innocents, for only doing what children do: be present. For being present during the worst moment of my life, for potentially being a distraction when my little brother died.

I continue to observe from Lawrence's point of view. I am stumbling around, noticing the piles and piles of papers, laundry, and random things. The floors are covered in things as well, and I am exploring. Picking up little pieces of whatever I can find. I examine everything.

I look up and see light. It is shining so brightly. I shield my eyes a bit to try to get a better look.

There is a large chair blocking the open doorway that leads to the backyard with a lot of stuff piled on top of it. It looks fun, like something to climb. I feel excitement rise in my tiny body.

I look back as I hear shouting coming from the kitchen. Kris and Steven's voices getting louder and louder. Something is happening. I see smoke coming from the kitchen. I can feel the distress in my bones.

Part of me wants to go back to see what is happening. The other children remain unfazed, continuing to laugh and play. *They are used to chaos.*

My attention drifts back to the partially barricaded doorway. The light from outside is streaming in above the mountain of random things separating me from my escape. The outside world calls me forward, begging me to engage. As my pudgy legs move me forward, the light streaming in from outside gets brighter and brighter. Suddenly, I am no longer being called outside toward freedom and fresh air; I am now being guided forward by this brilliant light. It calls me forward, and it feels strangely familiar. It feels like home.

I look down and notice I have already begun climbing on the chair mountain, ascending the piles of random things. I can hear myself letting out little, barely audible grunts as I climb, the light continuing to beckon me forward. *Why does this feel so familiar? Why does this feel like home?*

I fall to the other side of the chair mountain with a thud, the light getting brighter and brighter. I look around and notice that the light is coming from my grandparents' backyard. They live next door, and their yard is adjacent.

I cross the threshold between the backyards easily. I have done this many times since the fence is down, broken. There is no boundary between the backyards. The light continues to shine brightly between the broken parts of the fence. I continue to follow the light.

Once I get into my grandparents' backyard, I begin to realize that the light is coming from my grandparents' swimming pool. The light is sparkling and shimmering, seemingly alive, but it is not a reflection coming from the water. That is impossible. As I draw nearer to the pool, I see what I know was true about the day that Lawrence drowned. The pool is mostly drained except for a little murky green water stagnant at the bottom of the pool.

As I stumble closer and closer to the pool, my big toes hanging over the edge, the murky green water disappears and is replaced by the beautiful, flowing light. It's shimmering and dancing, and I am so intrigued. The feeling of being home continues to rise; I feel peace all over my body. With every step I take with my awkward, pudgy legs, I begin to feel more and more dread about what's next.

Be here now, I hear my brother repeat to me gently. I inhale deeply and allow myself to be led.

As I draw nearer and nearer to the pool, I begin to hear a beautiful chorus. Angels. The light becomes more brilliant as I draw near, and now I can see other colors sparkling in the light as well. Pinks and blues and greens, all dancing together amidst the ethereal music. I feel my body stumble as I fall physically into the pool. I know intellectually what is happening, but all I can sense is this overwhelming peace. I am no longer in the physical realm, and I am experiencing what my brother experienced at the end.

He is in water but not in his physical state. He is floating gently underwater as the angelic chorus continues to guide him forward. He is now bathed in this beautiful light, blues and pinks and greens swirling around and mixing with the water and light to create truly stunning art in motion.

I cannot tell exactly when his human life ends and when the in-between begins. All I know for sure is that he does not suffer at all. All he feels in his final moments are peace and feelings of being home.

I see a flash of bright light as everything suddenly gets quiet and still. I see his memories begin to flash in front of him. They are few because he is so young in this human existence, but I recognize a few of them. I see... *me*. As his Ate. I'm smiling and spinning him around. I'm laughing as he eats. I'm so joyful with him yet so deeply saddened under the surface. *I saw your suffering, Ate, and I always tried to make you smile,* Lawrence says. I smile, remembering how much joy he brought to my life when I was so lost, so sad. I still cannot bring myself to feel any grief or sadness in this present moment because everything is so stunning, seeing all of his memories, his *feelings,* from this life.

I sense intuitively that the life has come to a close, that the events and the memories have been recorded, and it is time to move forward. The light has returned, as well as the chorus of angels. I'm now observing Lawrence as he moves forward into the light and away from my consciousness. We are separate now, and he is absolutely stunning. He is an angel, which I already knew, but his body is no longer one of a child. He looks like a seasoned warrior, with long, blond hair flowing past his shoulders and armor covering his body. He is holding a shield and a large sword, both glowing with the same golden energy as the light that is calling him forward. His wings are large and shimmering white and pearlescent behind him. He expands them fully, and his wingspan is at least a dozen feet wide. I can't take my eyes off of him. He is magnificent. I watch him intently as he disappears into the bright light, and I am transported back to this current moment.

My son is playing in front of me, holding a tin lunchbox filled with dinosaurs. He is laughing and playing, seemingly unaware of the journey I just embarked upon.

I drop into my body and feel a deep sense of gratitude for having witnessed my brother's beautiful transition to the in-between. *You didn't suffer?* I ask my brother, whose spirit is still present with me.

No, he says. *I didn't.*

I guess I still don't understand why it had to happen, I say, which sounds more like a question than I intended.

We're not always meant to understand why, he replies. *However, Source would like me to explain something. Water can be healing, and water can be destructive. But water, at its core, is neutral. It is neither healing nor destructive. It simply IS. It exists, just like we all do. To view water, or anything really, as either healing or destructive is simply a matter of perspective. Water is neither and it is also both, and so much more. Yet water is neutral.*

I sense myself struggling to understand this concept, his words.

Be here now, Ate. This isn't a philosophical thought for the sake of understanding. This is information that is critical to your present mo-

ment in time.

I breathe deeply and quiet my thoughts, opening myself to the awareness that is trying to make its way to me. *Destruction is inevitable...* I say to Lawrence. *And often required.*

I'm transported to my grandparents' house in Florida again, yet this time, I am myself. I am sitting on the back patio, which is screened in, observing a fierce storm raging outside. *I remember this moment,* I say to Lawrence. *It was summer and we were visiting, and we were on the outskirts of a hurricane. I remember thinking how beautiful it all was, the destruction.* I continue to breathe, allowing myself to smell the piercing raindrops of the storm, to see the palm leaves and branches swirling in the unrelenting, harsh winds. In the distance, I see a bright flash of lightning and, moments later, I hear the loud crack of thunder. I can feel the water touching my skin, coming in through the screen.

I suddenly see memories from the last several months. Quitting my corporate job and speaking truth in every space I could before I left. *I caused destruction in leaving,* I say to Lawrence. *And, it was required. I also inspired growth. Awareness. Healing.*

I see Troy, our final fight before I left for my sister's house. *I blew up my marriage, my family,* I reflect quietly. *And, it was required. I needed to honor my whole self, my whole spirit, and I could no longer do so in that space as it was.*

I suddenly notice Finn has gotten suspiciously quiet. "Honey?" I call out as I look around.

I see him in the kitchen, two hands full of Nutella, stuffing his face. I laugh out loud as he smiles from ear to ear. "Yummy, Mama!" he says, holding both messy hands up for me to see. He had used his stepstool to reach the Nutella, which had been on the counter.

He's happier, I say as awareness continues to dawn on me. *Destruction was required because our fighting was not good for him either. Now Troy and I are both more at peace, apart.* I continue to reflect on the last couple of months, remembering how well Finn adjusted to the changes.

He adjusted easily because he's more peaceful as well, Lawrence says.

Water is neutral, I say again, awareness continuing to flow to me. *I am water. And I am neutral. I am nothing, and I am everything. I exist in this present moment, and I exist in all of time. I am all of it at once. I can be everything at once. I am pure consciousness. I am pure awareness. And awareness is not good or bad… it just IS. This is the paradox, OUR paradox, as humans. We are so much more expansive than we know. We have confined ourselves to these structures… to being one thing or another. We have made our identities mutually exclusive. We have placed judgment on every single thing in our lives, even our own emotions. And yet… we are only asked to exist in our expansiveness. We are only asked to be the highest, most unfettered versions of ourselves. When we play small, which so many of us are so used to doing every day of our lives… When we play small, we contribute to the collective suffering. We were never meant to play small. We were simply meant to BE.*

Suddenly, a song enters my mind: "After the Storm" by Mumford & Sons. It is a song that has gotten me through several breakups. *"There will come a time, you'll see… with no more tears… and love will not break your heart… but dismiss your fears. Get over your hill and you'll see… what you find there… with grace in your heart and flowers in your hair…"*

There is always a quiet calm after the storm, Lawrence says. *You just have to be willing to see it. And you will never see it if you focus on the storm, the storm that has already passed and is long gone. Too many are focused on the storm rather than the calm that comes afterward in the present moment.*

What does this mean for me? I ask, beginning to see the connections. *I see the constructs; I see the suffering. I see it all, as if I'm seeing it through Source's eyes.*

Source will bring humanity back to neutral, he says. *And you are the messenger. And the Uber driver.* I see my brother chuckle, and I smile. *You will bring them to the Truth.*

ALIGNING REALITIES

It is the morning of December 31, 2020, and I am just waking up after a mostly sleepless night. I roll over to glance at my alarm clock. 11:01 AM. I groan.

Troy and I are scheduled to meet in a couple of hours to talk about how we are both feeling about the separation. I have been dreading the conversation, sensing that it will likely be a fight. I have pictured how the conversation will go over and over in my head, and I wince every time I think about it. I will ask if he still plans to drink, and he will say yes. I will say that doesn't work for me. I will ask if he's willing to support my work, my spirituality. He will give me an answer that won't feel satisfactory for me. I will leave feeling as though nothing has come of the conversation, nothing is resolved. I will leave feeling unseen. I've played the scenario in my mind more times than I can count, and it's exhausting each time.

I sigh deeply and roll back over. I begin to contemplate the dream I was having just prior to waking up.

In this dream, I am frantic, desperately trying to pack a suitcase. I am running around a house I do not recognize, looking for my belongings, which are scattered all around. I feel so disorganized as several people I know, about a dozen friends of mine from completely different stages of my waking life, begin to make their way out the door, suitcases in hand. Through the bedroom window, I see them boarding what appears to be a large boat on an expansive body of water. The water stretches seemingly far past the horizon, and it sparkles vibrantly under the bright sun.

I know intuitively that this boat is taking us to the Dolomites, a majestic mountain range in Italy. In my waking life, the Dolomites are a special place for me. I traveled there five times over the course of five years in my late twenties and early thirties. This location is so sacred to me for the simple reason that so much of my emotional healing occurred there. It is *my place,* and it represents my journey of alignment with my higher self.

In my dream state, I am not making the connection. All I know is that I am frantically behind everyone else in being ready and still trying my best to pack the perfect bag. I am missing so many items, items that I feel are critical to my having the perfect experience. Perfection is a glaring theme in this dream.

I am close to finishing packing my suitcase when my glasses suddenly break and fall off my face. My anxiety spikes again as I bend down to pick up the glasses. I hold the frames in one hand and several screws and both lenses in the other hand. My heart is racing at this point as one of my friends calls to me from outside.

"Lani! Let's go! We have to leave now, or we're not going to arrive on time."

"I'm coming!" I respond. "My glasses broke and I'm trying to find a repair kit." I begin searching frantically for something to repair my glasses, my vision now blurry. The next thing I know, I am making my way to the boat, suitcase in hand.

"About time!" my friends tease, and I let out a sigh of relief as the boat pulls away from the dock.

I become aware that a few of my friends are actually men that, in my waking state, I have had feelings for at one point or another. I feel butterflies in my stomach as I see them. I am observing them, trying to speak with them, but they are consumed with other love interests. I am simply the 'good friend' that they are joking with and processing with, but they are romantically interested in other women. I feel myself working hard to get their attention, wishing that they would interact with me in the same ways that they did with these other women; however, they never do.

Then I wake up.

And now, looking back on the dream, tears begin to fill my eyes as awareness dawns on me. I pick up the phone to send a video message to Grace. I describe the dream to her and cry as I tell her what I became aware of in that moment.

"I never make it to the Dolomites, Grace," I say between sobs. "And I know what it means. The frantic packing, the seeking perfection, the men who don't love me… they were all distractions. They all kept me from the Dolomites, from becoming my whole self. I… I have to end my marriage today. I have to let go of Troy. He's keeping me from the Dolomites. He's keeping me out of my divinity." I continue to sob and more deeply now. I am grieving with my entire being, feeling the gravity of the statement I just made. "It hurts, friend… this hurts so bad. I still love him, and I have to let him go…"

I continue to sob, recording each epiphany, each awareness, until my sobs begin to quiet, and my breathing finally slows down.

"Thank you for always being on the other end, friend. I love you. I'll let you know how it goes." I push the button to end the video.

I lie back down in my bed, still feeling the grief in my bones as tears stream down my face. I pick up my phone to call my sister, Kris.

"Hey sister," she says as she picks up.

"Hey… you got a minute?" I say quietly. Her energy shifts immediately as she, no doubt, picks up on the emotion in my voice.

"Yeah, what's up?" she replies. I proceed to describe the dream and, this time, am able to hold it together a bit as I describe the conversation I need to have with Troy.

"Oh, Ate. That's so hard," she says. "But that dream… I mean, the Dolomites is where you found yourself. It's where you healed. And you can't do that right now in this relationship."

Tears continue to stream down my face as her words resonate with me. "I just… I thought that it would be a fight, but I don't think it will be. I think… I just need to end it. I need to move on so that I can become who I'm meant to be in this life."

"Take a shower, get grounded. Do what you need to do to get centered," she says. "Take good care of yourself before you have to do this. But know this: *you can do this*." She emphasized each word, as if energetically pushing the message to my soul.

"You're right. Thanks, sis. Love you." My breathing is calmer now as I feel her words sink into my awareness. I wipe the tears from my cheeks one last time.

"Love you. Call me later, let me know how it goes."

"Okay, bye." I hang up the phone and sigh deeply before sitting upright and standing up.

I walk into the bathroom and start the shower. I remove my clothes as I notice the steam rising above the shower curtain. I step in and immediately sit down in the tub. I used to do this all the time in my late twenties when I was deep in my trauma healing. I would sit in the shower, hugging my knees tightly toward my torso, and I would close my eyes and crane my head down, allowing the water to fall on the back of my head and run down the rest of my body. There was something so comforting about the position, and it called to me quickly in this moment.

As water flows through my hair, down my legs, and down the

drain, I suddenly notice I am no longer crying. I am simply… being.

I lift my face toward the water, something I don't typically do when I'm in this position. I open my mouth and feel surprised that I can still breathe. *I can breathe underwater,* I say silently to myself.

You are water, I hear a voice say. Source. *Remember, water is healing and destructive. And, at its root, water is neutral. It simply IS. It exists, and everything else is a matter of perspective.*

I breathe deeply, still clutching my knees, my face still upward and being pelted by water, as I internalize the truth in the moment. *I am water. I am destructive. I am healing. I am neutral.* I pick myself up off of the floor and stand, continuing to allow the water to fall on my face. *I am water.*

***

I am sitting in my car outside of Troy's house, my old house. It feels bizarre to be here. I feel out of place in the same way I felt out of place at my corporate role right before I left. Like an old skin that no longer fit. An empty shell which used to hold me and now is a collection of cells, dead skin, crumpled on the ground in front of me. *What do you do with an old skin?*

You honor it, I hear. Again, guidance from Source. *You thank it for all it has given you, all it has taught you. Your life as it is today would not exist without the people and experiences that have been a part of your journey. This old skin, it is a blessing. It deserves to be honored.*

Deep, intuitive awareness lights up my body as I breathe deeply and internalize the wisdom. Energy flows through my body like electricity, leaving goosebumps in its wake. After a moment, my energy settles, and I take a final breath before opening the car door.

I walk slowly toward the front door and knock gently before I use my key to enter.

"Hey," I call out as I enter the house, removing my shoes and placing them on the shoe rack by the front door.

"Hey, be right there," I hear Troy call from the family room.

I sit down at the dining room table and close my eyes, imagining an invisible barrier slowly surrounding me as I silently ask Source for strength to get my message across. I take a deep breath and see Troy sit down at the other end of the table.

"You want to go first?" I ask as I realize I am fidgeting with my hands. I quickly place them in my lap.

"You can go," he replies, his posture surprisingly open.

"Okay," I say, scrambling to find where to start. "I... I love my space," I blurt out, and he smiles. Relief washes over me as I see him grin, and I continue. "I love my space, I love my apartment, and I don't want to let it go. I've been feeling really grateful for you... really grateful... for the ways we have been able to navigate co-parenting, and...," I stop and breathe deeply before continuing. "I think we should call it."

His shoulders, which had tensed up as I spoke, ease down a bit as he exhales. "I'm relieved to hear you say that," he says, and I can actually hear the relief in his voice. "I feel the same way. I wasn't sure where you stood with everything."

"Oh, wow. I didn't expect that," I say, sitting back in my chair and exhaling. *Was I holding my breath?* "I really do think we are great co-parents, and good friends... but..."

"We're just so different," he finishes. "And I don't want to stifle you, this work that you're doing. I know I don't really get it... I'm not on the same page. I don't want to get in the way of what you want to do."

Hot tears begin to fall down my cheeks. *This is all such a relief,* I say silently, *and unexpected.* We continue talking about logistics and timing. We hash out details about Finn, about the house, finances. After ten or fifteen minutes of talking, we realize that we have covered pretty much everything. *This is the easiest conversation we may have ever had. It feels like the first time we have ever agreed on anything. We are completely aligned for once.*

And I am water, I process simultaneously as I feel us wrapping up the conversation. *I entered this conversation expecting to be destructive, and this is feeling so… neutral. It just is. I finally understand.*

I feel an emotion begin to bubble up from the center of my chest with a gentle ferocity that is difficult to ignore. As the conversation continues to wind down, I suddenly blurt it out.

"I still love you," I hear myself saying, and I immediately notice him cross his arms. "I'm sorry if that complicates things, but I do. I love you, and I am still really grounded in this decision. I think it's time we move on. We really tried, and this is the right move. But it was never about love. I have always cared about you."

He doesn't respond, and he appears visibly uncomfortable. I follow up quickly to spare him from further discomfort. "Thank you, Troy," I say as I step toward him and hug him. He seems to welcome the embrace and hugs me back tightly.

He chuckles. "Well, that was easy!" I sense overwhelming relief radiating from him.

"That *was* easy!" I laugh. "Have you been on any dating sites?" I ask, teasingly, a smirk finding my lips.

"No… but now I will be," he says, and I laugh heartily. It feels appropriate to leave the relationship this way. It's how we met—laughing and playing and having fun.

"Take care, Troy," I say, meaning it with every fiber of my being.

"You, too," he responds with a smile.

And just like that, I am gone.

***

Later that day, I am sitting cross-legged on my yoga mat on my living room floor facing the large sliding glass door that leads to my balcony. I look out and see the cars driving on the street below, the trees lining the road. It's a clear day, and I can see the Olympic mountains in the distance. Everything feels right in this moment and yet, also so… unresolved.

I take a deep breath and close my eyes. *There's a message here…* I think to myself.

I feel my breath enter my lungs and I breathe out deeply, slowly. An emotion begins to arise, beginning in my belly. Sadness.

In my mind's eye, I see polaroid pictures begin to take form. They are my favorite memories with Troy.

A candid photo from our wedding day of my eyes closed and a soft smile on my face, my head resting on his shoulder as he kisses my forehead.

The photo from the day of Finn's birth, the first moment I held him. He's crying in the photo, but Troy and I are so joyful, grins spread widely across our faces. We finally get to meet him. We finally know our son.

A picture from a party we attended where we were both laughing hysterically. Us in our deepest joy before the worst of times.

I feel tears forming in my eyes as I continue to see our most sacred memories flashing across my mind's eye, and I begin to anticipate what is next. *We have to dissolve these memories, don't we? I have to let these go in order to heal?*

I begin to notice another shape taking form. Light brown leather with tan stitching. A suitcase. The suitcase opens and the beautiful Polaroids begin to pour into the suitcase one by one.

The grief continues to pull at me, and I begin to cry, my face cradled in my hands, knowing what is next. However, something I did not expect happens: the suitcase closes, and it is placed in my hand.

You get to take these with you, I hear Source say with conviction. *These memories, these lessons. They are now a part of your soul's journey. You must let go of the possibilities with Troy in this lifetime, but you get to keep the joy, the love, the lessons. And you get to carry them with you for many lifetimes to come.*

I am sobbing with my whole body now, relief washing over me in giant waves. This moment is important for so many reasons, but what is bubbling to the surface is the deep relief that I don't have to forget what this relationship meant to me, to our family, to my soul's journey. *This experience… it wasn't for nothing then. I get to learn from this. I get to carry these memories with me.*

You do, Source responds gently. *And no, this experience wasn't without meaning. There is always purpose. There is always meaning.*

EMERGING

The next day, after I put Finn down for bed, I make my way back to my room and lie down in my own bed. I lean over to my bedside stand and click on the projector, and it instantly begins to glow on the ceiling above, a swirling landscape of blue night sky and stars. I breathe in deeply and click a few buttons on my phone, putting my favorite playlist on shuffle.

The music begins gently playing and I continue to breathe deeply. I have been reading about shamanism over the last several days, and I have come to the realization that the way I have been moving through space and time is actually shamanic journeying. In this moment, I am feeling called to journey, so I breathe deeply and allow whatever is meant for me to know in this moment to come forward.

The song that is playing is called, "Step Outside," by José González, and I smile as I see my little brother, Lawrence, come forward. I give him a hug, and he takes my hand in his. I hear the music faintly wafting in the distance as he pulls me forward. We begin running toward a faint light in the expanse, and I look over at him and notice that he has suddenly grown much taller,

236

much older. Right before my eyes, he has transformed into the same grown, muscular warrior from earlier, his brilliant wings outstretched behind him, and his long, flowing blond hair falling past his shoulders. He is truly beautiful in this state, stunning.

We run faster and faster toward the light as the music continues to crescendo, laughing joyfully, our hands still clasped together. Just as the music reaches its peak, the light transforms into a beautiful, glowing white orb, and Lawrence and I jump in headfirst.

The music is surrounding us now, mixing with the divine energy, and I am floating, weightlessly, as though in a bubble of water. *I can breathe…* I think to myself. *I am water. I am home.*

I am healed.

I continue to swim in the beautiful energy, laughing and playing with Lawrence, observing him as his higher self. He is a beautiful warrior. So weathered and so wise. I can sense that his soul is much older than mine.

You get to be at peace, Ate, he says with a boyish grin. *You get to be joyful. You get to be light. You are all things, and you are nothing, all at once. Embrace your divinity fully. It's time to step out.*

WHAT IS REAL?

The next day, I am making updates to my website when I see a notification pop up. It's an email from Lynz, my podcast producer and editor.

> Hi Leilani,
> Your podcast trailer is now LIVE in all the places! Still aiming for a January 7 drop date for Episode 1.
> Happy sharing!
> Lynz

"YAY!" I say out loud and jump up out of my computer chair. I dance in place for a few moments and Finn joins me, excitedly picking up on my joyful energy. I pick up my phone and begin crafting a message to post on my social media account. *People have been waiting for this…* I assure myself, suddenly feeling a bit self-conscious.

Suddenly, my inner critic chimes in. *Who are you to host a podcast? To get this message out? Do you really think people will like this? It's for a very specific set of people…* My ego is running wild.

I push the thoughts aside and hit "Post" on my phone. I smile as I look down at the podcast art, a bright yellow and indigo design, representing the solar plexus and third eye chakras. White circles envelop the podcast title: *The Intuitive Activist*. A small triangle with an eye in the center of it. I designed the podcast art in December with a little help from my intuitive friends, and it was completely channeled. Seeing the art and my corresponding post gives me a sense of ease as I put my phone aside and focus back on my computer.

I begin scrolling through a few business invoices and notice I need to pay one of my contractors. A few clicks later, I open a window showing my bank account, and my jaw drops when I notice my personal bank account balance: $5,000.12.

Oh, shit, I think to myself. *How is that possible?*

Just a few short weeks prior, my account balance was a little under $15,000 after receiving the severance check from my corporate job. After paying down some debt, as well as various business invoices, that balance seems to have quickly depleted.

Sharp and familiar panic begins to rise in my chest. I sit down and begin to breathe deeply and allow the anxiety to subside, but the fear still looms under the surface, like the quiet static of a radio turned down low but not off. It nags at me for the rest of the evening, completely distracting me as Finn continues to pull at me for my attention.

I find myself feeling more and more emotionally raw and depleted; I see myself snap at Finn. "No, please stop!" I say firmly, and I look down at him, truly noticing him for the first time in about an hour. He had been pulling at my pants, begging to be picked up, when I snapped. I had been so consumed in my own despair that I hadn't noticed the ways in which I was neglecting him.

In this moment, he is looking up at me as his arms fall to his sides. Tears form in his eyes as his lower lip begins to quiver.

"Oh, honey," I say as I drop to my knees to give him a hug. "I'm so sorry, baby." He begins to let out a wail, undoubtedly releasing the emotion of not having my attention that had been building up in his tiny body all day.

I need support… I'm losing my mind… I think. I pick up my phone and send a video message to Grace.

"Hi friend, I just need to say this out loud. I have $5,000 to my name right now and I'm really afraid about money…" I go on to describe the circumstances and my fear around my dwindling account balance. "I'm just feeling so overwhelmed, empty."

I tap the button to end the recording and proceed with putting Finn down for bed. I spend a bit of extra time rocking with him and singing to him, trying my best to make up for the ways I could not be present with him earlier in the day. Finally, I tuck him in, turn off the light, and leave his room.

When I return to the living room, I notice my phone buzz. I pick it up to view the notification: a video message from Grace.

"Hi friend," Grace says. "I connected with your energy while accessing the akashic records. I wanted to see if there was anything I could do to support you. Here's what I saw… I saw a swimming pool, which had been drained, with full roses which were still wet from the recently drained water."

My breath catches in my throat as my grandfather's pool comes to mind. When Lawrence drowned, the pool was mostly drained as well. My attention snaps back to Grace's message.

"…I saw you flailing around at the bottom of the pool, almost as if you were trying to swim, but there was no water. I think the water signified wealth, which wasn't there in that moment because the pool had been drained. And you were flailing so you didn't immediately realize the beauty that was still surrounding you."

I begin to notice I'm sobbing at this point. I wipe away tears with my sleeve as I continue to focus on the vision that Grace is describing.

"Once you stopped flailing a bit, you were able to stand up and realize the beauty that surrounded you; it was all around you. You stopped trying to swim in something that wasn't there.

"After that, you and I walked together to a healing pool, and we both dove in and swam around in it a bit. We both needed healing in that moment, and we were able to laugh and swim together. Our kids were also attached to us, and I honored that they are part of our journeys right now.

"After we left the healing pool, we were walking home. It was really dark, but you were holding a flashlight. It was small, but it was bright. It was enough light to guide us home…"

Grace's message continues, but I am sobbing so deeply at this point, that it is difficult to make out the words. *She's helping me heal… I'm healing in this moment, aren't I?*

Yes, I hear a voice confirm. I know instantly that it's Source. *There's no water in the pool. There is no way you can drown.* I pick up my phone to respond to Grace.

"Thank you, friend," I say between sobs. "That vision… it was so impactful. I am so grateful you shared it with me. I don't know if I told you this, but my little brother drowned in a mostly drained pool. So when you were describing it to me, it looked to me like it was happening in my grandfather's pool. The thought of that drudged up a lot of grief for me but also healing, which captures most of this journey for me.

"And I just really appreciate your willingness to support me. You knew what I needed… even though you kind of didn't know, you knew.

"This journey continues to feel so expansive. Holding so many opposites all at once…" I suddenly remember Finn was in the vision as well, and I begin sobbing again. "And Finn… I'm just so afraid, friend… I'm so afraid I'm going to let him down, that I will let everyone down, that I will let Source down…" I am now sobbing with my entire spirit. I inhale deeply, let it out slowly, and continue. "And the light… I felt that with my entire being. It looked so small at first, and I thought, 'What am I supposed to do with this?' Then I turned it on and it was like a floodlight. It was so bright, that it didn't even seem dark at all anymore." I pause, allowing tears to fall down my cheek. "I know I'm a guide. I know I am. I know I'm guiding people with my light, toward home. And… being a guide is really fucking hard sometimes. It's lovely and fulfilling so much of the time, and it's really hard sometimes. I know I'm a key… one of many keys… but a key nonetheless. And sometimes the mission feels too big, too hard. But knowing you're walking with me, knowing I'm not alone… it means so much. I need you, and I need my community.

"What I'm hearing now is… I can trust myself. I can trust my intuition. I cannot fail; it's not possible. Without fear, there is no courage. And if there's something I know about myself, it's that I'm fucking courageous. I know courage. I know valor. I know how to fulfill my mission. I've done it for lifetimes, and I'll do it again here and now.

"Thank you again, Grace. I appreciate you more than you know." I hit the button to end the message and move wearily to my bedroom. I slip under my comforter, which feels cool against my warm, flushed skin, and fall into a deep sleep.

THE ROOT OF FEAR

Over the course of the following two weeks, I anxiously witness my bank account balance continue to fall as I pay business, child-care, and living expenses. It is now 11 days until the end of the month. 11 days until rent is due. And I don't have the money to pay it. Not even close.

It is evening, and I kiss Finn goodnight. "I love you, honey. Sweet dreams…"

"Sweet *dweams*, Mama. *Yuv you*."

I walk out of the room and close the door quietly before opening the banking app on my phone for about the tenth time today. *Staring at the balance won't make it bigger…* I think to myself, feeling familiar shame wash over me. *How could I let this happen? I'm smarter than this. Expanding this business… was it too soon? Did I leave my corporate role prematurely? I'm so afraid…*

This fear. It has been the murky water that I have been wading in for several weeks now. Fears around money, around not being able to care for my son in the ways that he deserves. Fears that I cannot live a life of purpose while simultaneously providing a life for my son that I can feel proud of. The fear is paralyzing.

And the worst part is… I see myself swimming in it, and I *know* it's not helpful. I sense that I am getting in my own way, my fear blocking the abundance that is trying so desperately to make its way to me. I know with intuitive certainty that it is on its way, and yet… here I am. Paralyzed in my fear and drowning in my shame.

There's nothing left to do, I think to myself, *but surrender. But how? How do I release the fear? I don't know how to get out of my own way…*

You're not alone, one of my guides says.

I consider the thought for a moment. *Yes, that's true… I need support.*

I turn on the shower, remove my clothes, and toss them in the hamper. By the time I enter the shower, it is hot and steaming. I let the hot water fall onto my face as I sigh out heavily. *I need support,* I repeat to myself.

Ten minutes later, I step out of the shower and grab the white, fluffy towel hanging on the rack. It smells of lavender laundry detergent. I wrap it around me and finish my bedtime routine before putting on a cozy, oversized t-shirt and lounge pants and climb into bed.

Lying on my back, hands open and turned up to the ceiling, I begin to speak aloud, hoping that someone or something in the etheric realm can help.

"Please help me journey in my dreams tonight," I say, eyes closed and awaiting a response. I hear none. "I have to release this fear. I need to heal whatever is in the way of abundance. Please provide me with some support… help me process this… heal this. I don't know what else to do. Help me surrender, please. I am so grateful for you all. I love you."

I turn to lay on my right side and sigh deeply before drifting off to sleep.

The next thing I know, I am in my dream state. My dream is incredibly vivid – bright colors, solid structures. *Not a dream,* I think to myself, as awareness begins to make its way to me. I look around and see Troy.

"Oh, hey!" I say, waving, and he grins, waving back. Suddenly, I see a woman step out from behind him and grab his hand. She is short and looks very… plain. Pale hair. Pale skin. She pushes a lock of her light hair behind an ear and looks down. She is timid. Insecure. Unsure of herself. My antithesis. I instantly feel a tinge of… what? *What is this?* Judgment.

I see my friend, Arham, and I quickly begin talking about the woman. "I just can't believe he would go for her… doesn't seem like his type…" We exchange a few snarky, judgmental comments before transitioning to the next phase of the dream state, which feels more like a dream than the journeying that I just experienced.

When I wake in the morning, I am still thinking of the exchange and my immediate judgment, my unkind gossiping. *Reality. It's sinking in,* I say to my spirit guides, and I notice nods of confirmation in my mind's eye. *I'm… sad.*

Tears sting my eyes as awareness continues to rise within me, threatening to envelope me in her waves. *This is grief,* I state silently. *The fear…? The money…? It wasn't the root of the issue, was it?*

No, I hear, and I allow the tears to fall freely as I consider that.

I'm sad. I'm grieving. It feels heavy today, I continue.

Yes, they say. *This is required. Breathe through it.*

As my sobs become louder and tears roll down my cheeks, I continue to process the healing that is occurring in this present moment. It was never about money. The root of the fear was this grief, my sadness, my letting go. *Is this all my fault? Have I failed?* The self-deprecating thoughts are something that Josette describes as a phantom habit. It's an old defense mechanism, something from an old way of being, that doesn't reflect who I know I am today. However, today, in all of my humanness, I feel it all. The sadness. The grief. The guilt. The feelings of failure. I am immersed in my emotions when I feel my phone buzz. I look down to see my sister, Kris, calling me. I push the button to connect.

"Hey," I say a bit absently, still feeling distracted and panicked about my financial woes.

"Hey… I'm feeling some things. You got a minute?"

I listen to her describe a difficult work situation. As I hear the emotion rising in her voice, I instinctively shift into my Ate role and try my best to concentrate on her dilemma. After talking through it with her a bit, she sighs, and I sense that she has experienced a bit of relief.

"How about you? How is everything going?" she asks inquisitively.

"Well, I've been worried… about money," I start and catch her up on all of the worries I have been processing over the last few weeks.

She pauses before responding. "Can I offer something for you to try?"

"Yes, of course," I ask, genuinely interested in her suggestion.

"Well, when I am feeling overwhelmed with my thoughts, my anxieties, I connect with my body. I put on some calming music, draw a bath with Epsom salts and allow my body to sink. I take some deep breaths and allow my breath to draw me back up, right before the water completely engulfs me. It requires that I let go and be present."

"Hm…," I say, thinking about her suggestion. "Sure, I mean… I'll try anything at this point."

"Yeah… I'm getting a strong intuitive sense that you need to do this tonight," she says. "You know I got you, right? I love you."

"I know. I love you, too," I say, smiling, and we hang up.

***

Later that evening, I fill the bathtub as instructed and start playing music from a playlist entitled "Tibetan singing bowls." I hang my robe on the hook behind the door before stepping into the hot bath. I see steam rising from the water as I sink into it, light flames flickering from the cashmere-scented candles all along the edge of the tub.

I empty my lungs completely and feel my body instinctively begin to panic as my face becomes almost completely submerged. My nose is still above the water and I breathe in fully, allowing my lungs to bring my body back to the surface. I do this several times and eventually become increasingly confident that I will not become submerged.

In my confidence, I feel my thoughts begin to wander to money again. *What if I pursued more consulting bids? Do I need to file for unemployment?*

Suddenly, water rushes up my nose, and I am jolted up, coughing and spitting salt water. "What the hell?" I say, still in shock. *What just happened?*

You left the present moment, I hear my guides say. *Be here now.*

After a few moments, I relax fully back into the water. My breathing becomes rhythmic, inhaling as I rise to the surface, exhaling as I sink back toward the bottom of the tub.

Suddenly, everything feels quiet, expansive. I could hear a pin drop. *Fear doesn't belong here,* I think. *I can't actually drown. My body will keep me safe.*

And, my guides add, *leaving the present moment is not benign. It will always rob you of your peace. Peace exists only in this present moment, the only moment that truly exists.*

SURRENDERING

The following day, I am answering emails on my computer when I realize I haven't stood up for several hours. I stand up and stretch my arms above me, breathing in and filling my lungs before letting everything out and allowing my arms to drop to my side.

I walk to the kitchen and pour myself a glass of water. As I take a sip, I find my mind wandering to my finances once again. *When will my next client payment arrive? What bills are coming due...? Rent... utilities... insurance. Argh. I know I don't have enough in my bank account to pay all of that...*

Suddenly, I notice Jesus in my mind's eye. "Oh, hey, J!" I say playfully. He rolls his eyes.

You're ridiculous, he replies with a grin. His expression softens. *You know you can give all of that to me, right? All that you're worried about?*

"Ugh...," I start, feeling annoyed that I still have not released my fears around money.

Just give it to me, really, he assures me. *I can handle it.*

"Okay, fine!" I smile, thinking about everything that has been weighing heavy on my heart. "All of my financial worries! Here, take it!" As I say it, I imagine tossing a giant boulder over to him.

What else? he says with a soft smile.

"Oh, I don't know… how about my divorce? Finn? All of the ways there is potential to screw up our kid because we couldn't figure out how to stay married?!" I laugh. Jesus continues to smile back at me, remaining steady. Expectant.

Well? he says calmly. *Is that it? Really? That's nothing.* Suddenly, I notice he is hooked up to a carriage, and he is at the front, pretending as though he is the horse pulling it. The carriage is huge, like a giant, ancient U-Haul. I laugh audibly. The message he is trying to convey to me is clear: he can take on a lot. I don't have to worry about burdening him.

I list a few more of my worries in between laughs and finally feel as though I don't have anything else to give over. "I mean, I guess that's it. Otherwise, my life is pretty great! Can I just start listing things for which I'm grateful?"

Please do! Jesus replies.

"Well, there's Troy. I'm grateful we have been able to co-parent so well and that the relationship has been so peaceful lately. Co-operative. There is common respect and understanding, and we both prioritize Finn's experience.

"And then there's Finn, of course," I continue. "He's thriving. He seems to be adapting so well and seems so much calmer and well-adjusted now. And I'm just so grateful that I get to be his mom!

"I have an amazing apartment, food in the fridge, and still have money in my bank account. We've never actually been in a situation where we haven't had enough. I have an incredible job, supportive friends and family. I mean…," I hesitate. "All is well."

Jesus smiles back at me. *Sounds like you're pretty happy. Life is pretty good,* he says lovingly. He's still hooked up to the giant, old-timey carriage, and I giggle.

"Yeah. Life is pretty great," I say, allowing myself to breathe into that truth. "Wow, I feel so much better!" I laugh.

He smiles back at me. *Funny how that works, huh?* He begins to walk, taking the carriage with him. I laugh.

"You are so funny! But… thank you. Seriously, J. I love you."

He smiles. *Love you, sis.* And he is gone.

I drink a bit more water and sit back down at my desk. I see an email from one of our clients and click on it to open it.

Hi Leilani!

Attached is the signed contract. Let me know if you need anything else.

Thanks for your partnership!

-E

I open the attachment, even though I already know the value of the contract. I just need to see the signed contract with my own two eyes.

"Oh my gosh… it *is* signed. $84,000." I stare in disbelief, allowing my brain to catch up to what I'm seeing. I gave my troubles over to Jesus literally minutes ago, and now I have a contract in front of me that completely releases me of my financial troubles. The first payment is due on the 1st, which, coincidentally, is when rent is due. "Whoa. I can't make this shit up."

There is no such thing as coincidence. This is all part of the plan, I hear my guides say. *You are seen. You are supported. We won't let you fall.*

44

CHOICES

Later that evening, I pull on my pajamas and crawl into bed. I find myself still processing a bit of residual fear, wondering why, if I now feel as though money will come, fear is still surfacing. I am so frustrated and feel powerless, and I energetically reach toward my guides for answers.

You must heal, I hear Source say. *You have to journey back to your most fearful moment. You must heal it.*

I am jarred by a flashback of an old memory. I am six years old in our old kitchen, pushing a broom slowly and mindlessly.

"No…," I say aloud, my hands shaking. Tears sting my eyes. "No, I can't. It's too scary. I'm not strong enough. I… I can't…"

You can, Source says, gently interrupting my despair. *You won't be alone. I will be with you. You are safe, and you are protected. I will never let you fall.*

Tears are falling freely from my eyes now, and my gaze snaps toward my bedroom window as I notice a sudden and bright flash of light. Moments later, thunder cracks loudly and angrily, shaking the windowpane in its wake. I sigh deeply as I lay my head on my pillow and pull the comforter up to my chin.

"Okay," I say. I feel old emotions wash over me and notice my body instinctively already beginning to journey back to the memory. *My body knows what it's doing...* I think to myself. I pick up my phone, open the voice memo app, and hit the button to record and set it next to me. I close my eyes and begin speaking aloud.

It's been storming all night. The rain is coming down in sheets, and the lights began to flicker about an hour ago.

I'm overcome with fear. I'm not in control of anything. I'm disconnected. I'm afraid. Afraid that I made the wrong choices. That I let go of stability and security.

I'm afraid.

My guides are asking me when I've been the most afraid.

I'm transported, moving through space and time. I'm six years old. I'm in the kitchen, pushing a broom around. Slowly. Mindlessly.

I was told to clean up. To finish my chores.

My siblings are playing in the room together. He told them to stay there or else they would get in trouble. They're just playing.

I look down at the broom shaking in my hands. I can't stall any longer. I can't. I want to, but I can't.

Tears fall from my eyes. I wipe them away quickly as I've been conditioned to do.

I'm so afraid. I know what he does to me in there.

I'm afraid. I'm afraid that if I don't do it, he'll hurt us more.

I'm afraid that if I don't do it, he'll hurt my sisters the same way he hurts me.

The wind is howling. The windows are shaking here in this present moment threatening destruction.

I am in both places at once. I am in both bodies at once. I am expansive and the storm is raging all around me and also within me. All at once.

I am in the center of the Universe.

As I begin to walk down the hallway, I notice a cape of stars shim-

mering behind me, gently dragging on the floor.

I see my sister peering out. She looks afraid. "Something's not right, Ate. Something's not right." I walk to her.

"Thank you for seeing me. I didn't think anybody noticed.

"You don't have to cry.

"You don't have to cry.

"There is always... hope.

"Go play. Be a kid. You're safe. You're seen and you're known.

"I know you're afraid. You're protected. We all are. We're safe. Wipe your tears. I'll be back. I'm never going to leave you."

I kiss her forehead and I turn to walk down the hall. I hear the door close behind me. Click. She is safe.

With every step, the floor glows beneath my feet. I'm no longer touching the ground; I'm floating. My wings outstretched behind me. I'm carried with the strength of my entire spirit team; they have always been with me. Always. Playing with me. Teaching me. Even when I haven't seen them, they have been there. Providing subtle guidance, reminding me that there is always hope. There is always hope. It is always darkest before the dawn.

I step. Every step light beneath my feet, my cape of stars growing brighter and more brilliant, now floating behind me. My wings are shimmering, reflecting the light that is now streaming in through cracks in the ceiling. The cracks expand as the ceiling begins to crumble above me, exposing more of the heavens than ever before. The light is almost blinding, flooding in from gaping holes in the ceiling. I smile.

There is divinity here in this moment.

I am present.

I am no longer a little girl. I am my highest self.

The wind is howling, the rain is pattering against the windowpane, threatening destruction. Threatening damage. This is the point in which there is potential for destruction. This moment is primed for it.

I enter the room.

Disgust fills my body as I see that he has already removed his cloth-ing. He sees me as a child, yet I am no longer a child. I am a warrior.

With my shield and my sword, I could slay him. Effortlessly. With a flick of my wrist, I could cut off his head and put it on my mantle as a trophy. I could destroy him. In my bones and in my flesh, I have the power to destroy him.

The wind is howling. Rain threatening destruction. I carry the pow-er of my ancestors, my spirit team, the Universe itself.

I. Could. Slay. You.

And I pause.

Anger and disgust are melting away, leaving my body and return-ing to the Earth.

Water is trickling down the windowpane, gently, like veins. I've al-ways been fascinated by that. The way that the water moves on the windows like little roadways, meeting other paths and converging. Diverging.

There are creatures all around me. There is life, energy flowing through the structures we've created. These buildings. These intricate systems.

The house breathes. Inhaling and exhaling. Everything is alive. Energy is flowing through me, flooding my veins. I'm standing here, head cocked to one side. I'm looking at this man who sees a child be-fore him.

Suddenly, I smile as I notice awareness dawning on him. No longer a child he sees. She has transformed. She is powerful. He is fearful. Afraid of being slain by her sword and her shield.

He is fearful. All that he could lose. This little girl's oppressor now shaking. Quaking. Fearful.

She draws power from the walls and her spirit animals, her team and her ancestors. Drawing power and seeing it flow like water into her hands. Light and water, energizing her hands now, crackling with energy.

She. Is. In. Control.

She is the phoenix rising. Anger boiling under her skin. Anger from hundreds and hundreds of years. Lives lived. Oppression and death. What is the meaning of it all?

I. Am. In. Control.

Drawing power from the water that runs through the pipes under the house. The house breathing in and exhaling, breathing out.

There is power here. She is thirsty for it. She wants nothing more than to strike her oppressor with the full force of hundreds of years of oppression. Of playing small.

She is no longer fearful. She is powerful. She is in control of this very moment.

She breathes in unison with the house. Breathing out audibly.

She continues to pull on the energy of the house, and she suddenly notices an orb of light forming between her hands. Breathing in with the house. Breathing out with the house. The energy continues to crackle as electricity moves from one hand to the other, like small flashes of lightning traveling within her, feeding this orb, which is growing larger and larger with each passing moment.

Her oppressor is crying now, begging for mercy, though he knows in his heart he deserves none. His life flashes before his eyes. Years and years and years of oppression. Of hurt. Of bullying. Of feeling unseen. Of feeling unloved.

She approaches him, and he cowers, shaking with fear. He is holding his knees like a little boy, like the coward that he is. Rocking back and forth. He knows what's next. He deserves to be destroyed.

She continues to draw power and energy from the walls. Breathing in unison with the house.

The Universe twinkles behind her, her cape flowing gently, swept up in the storm.

She places a hand on each of his shoulders. He bows his head, awaiting destruction. She looks to the heavens, asking Source to move through her, surrendering her free will to the will of the Universe.

Eyes closed, she moves her hands from his shoulders to the center of his chest. His heart, once charred and black, now shines a bright white under her healing hands. The shadow of his heart is cast out and begins to ripple throughout his body as he fills with more and more light.

She brings her hands back in preparation for the final blow and moves her hands swiftly to the center of his chest, knocking him into the wall.

A dark shadow moves from his body and falls to the ground, making its way through the floorboards and returning to the Earth. Evil cast away.

He looks up, amnesiac. Confused. He looks around. "Where am I? What year is it?"

"You are seen," she says. "You are known. There is always hope. Rest, child."

I am in between dimensions. I walk between worlds. I'm a vessel of light. Bearer of divine truth. Gatherer of angels. Beacon for good. Lighthouse for the lost and the weary.

We are not alone. There is so much more beyond what we, as humans, deem as truth.

We are so capable. We are spiritual royalty. We belong to one another. We belong to Source. We are protected.

There is no fear.

This is all an illusion.

Breathe into the pain. Anxiety serves a purpose. Fear serves a purpose.

But trust... we are never alone. We never were.

I look to my oppressor. He is sobbing, beginning to remember all of the ways in which he allowed evil to reside within him. This was a choice. He is begging for forgiveness.

"Don't ask me for forgiveness," I reply. "I'm not the one."

I walk out of the room and free my siblings from their prison. I tell them we're leaving.

"We're going to the neighbors' house. We're telling them everything."

45

BECOMING

It is 2:25 AM, and tonight is the first full moon of 2021. I keep seeing images in my mind's eye of burning paper, and I know that my guides are telling me to release tonight. There is something powerful about actually releasing in the physical realm, and my guides are reminding me that tonight in particular, it will be important to do so.

I sit down at my desk and sigh deeply. I pick up a sheet of paper and tear it into several smaller pieces. On one of the small pieces of paper, I write: "I am free of…" I close my eyes and allow breath to fill my lungs, willing the words to move through me.

"I am free of fear and scarcity around money." That is the easy one, the explicit fear that I have been facing for several weeks. I fold the paper in half and then in half again so that it is a quarter of its original size before picking up another small piece of torn paper.

"I am free of…," I feel breath move into my body, "…control." I fold it in the same manner and set it aside. I pick up another piece of paper.

"I am free of…" The words begin to write themselves now, "…the false narrative that I don't know how to be a good mom."

"I am free of self-judgment and judgment from others."

"I am free of undervaluing myself."

"I am free of victimhood."

"I am free of…," I wait a moment before writing the last words of the evening, "…playing small."

I pick up all of the small folded pieces of paper and a lighter and walk toward the sliding glass door that leads to the balcony. I unlock the door and slide it open, and I immediately wince as a blast of cold air greets me suddenly. I step forward anyway, barefoot on my balcony, clutching the small pieces of paper in my left hand. I crouch down and set the papers on the floor of the balcony, and pick up one of the pieces and the lighter. There is a large metal bowl filled with rain water already on the balcony, and although the full moon itself is hidden behind an overcast sky, I sense its powerful, cleansing energy in the water. I see the word "control" peeking out from an opening on the side of the folded piece of paper, and I flick the lighter, putting the paper toward the flame. It catches easily, effortlessly, and it is consumed in a bright orange flame quickly. I wait until the paper is mostly ash before tossing it into the bowl of water. I hear a faint *hissss* as the water extinguishes the flame just as quickly as it caught fire.

I continue to ignite the pieces of paper, letting go of any attachment I had to any of the concepts from which I am declaring freedom. I am overwhelmed with an emotion that grows stronger with each charred piece of paper that I toss in the water charged with the moon's energy. I find myself oddly curious about the emotion as it continues to inhabit more and more of my physical body with each paper that is burned away then cleansed. It is an echo of lives past, an echo deep in my spirit. It is a part of me.

This feeling… it is empowerment. I am deeply powerful, divinity embodied. I am powerful in this moment and I always have been. In this present moment, I am finally remembering.

"And I'm not the only one," I say to myself. I think of the person reading this book, holding my story in their hands. They, too, are filled with such incredible, enormous power that is just begging to be discovered… yearning to be remembered.

In this moment, I hold space in my being for all of the people whom I have met along the way of my soul's journey as well as those I have yet to meet. I hold space for all of those who know in the depths of their spirit that there is so much more to this beautiful existence, so much more than what we are sensing with our eyes, ears, mouths, and skin.

We, as a collective, are so much more than what we have been allowing ourselves to be. Source is urging us to ascend, to pick up our arms and fight for good. Fight for hope.

As I ignite the final piece of paper, I notice words peeking out of the side: "…playing small." I breathe deeply, allowing myself to release the false notion that I was ever small as the flames swallow the paper quickly. The fire reaches my fingertips with such speed that I laugh as I toss the flaming paper into the water. The flame sits atop the water for a moment before slowly extinguishing with a faint *hissss*.

I place my right hand over my heart, honoring the moment and all of the guidance that has flowed my way over the past five months. All is well in this moment, and my journey is only beginning. I rise to my feet, suddenly feeling a surge of electricity in my legs. I take note of how the power is manifesting in my physical body at this point in time.

I slide the glass door open to re-enter my apartment. Somehow, the lights in the apartment seem brighter, the air lighter and fresher.

I smile as I hear angels singing in the etheric realm, celebrating my emergence. Their words and their music fill my spirit as I step back into my apartment, and I receive a faint image of stepping through a portal that feels eerily familiar yet oddly comforting.

Welcome home, dear one, I hear my guides say. *Rest up. You have work to do.*

EPILOGUE:

POST-DESTRUCTION REFLECTIONS

April 24, 2021

Dear One,

I am now several months removed from completing my manuscript and currently in the process of preparing for production. I come into this space today incredibly reflective, walking this now-beaten path, the path I have walked over and over but am just recognizing that I am able to see clearly for the first time, perhaps ever. This is the path of destruction and the path that is required to move forward into the life I am actively creating for myself.

There is a clearing that must happen, a scorching of the Earth. It's required in order to create space for new growth, for a new path. This inevitable destruction... it's a step that we so often want to rush through to keep us from feeling the impact of it all, whether that impact is within ourselves or whether it's the collateral damage we leave in our wake. This book has been an opportunity for me to sit in that destruction, to marinate in it. To swim in it and sink into it in ways that I have never allowed myself to do prior to this moment.

One of the many benefits of sinking so intentionally into the destruction we initiate is the healing that occurs as a result. Destruction is dark. It's messy. It's the terrifying unknown. We don't know what is on the other side of destruction and that fact alone keeps us in our comfort. It keeps us small, and it keeps us avoiding destruction at all costs. For some of us, this avoidance becomes our grayscale existence for our entire lives. For others like myself, it is a portion of our lives. But we all know what it feels like to avoid destruction because of the fear of the unknown, what inevitably lies on the other side of it.

I am here today to tell you how beautiful post-destruction can be. 2020 was a year of blowing up my life as I knew it, and it was the most terrifying thing I have ever done. And the beauty that I have experienced and continue to experience on the other side of the terrifying unknown is the most striking and utterly magnificent landscape I have witnessed to date.

And I beg you, please don't look at me like some anomaly. "Oh, she's just really brave. I could never be that brave. I couldn't possibly."

No.

Because while courage is required to walk into the depths of the unknown, the fear-inducing "in-between," it is not all that is required.

My community has sustained me. My belief in and hope for humanity has sustained me. My spiritual connection has sustained me.

All of these things have mixed and melded to create a beautiful storm of grief. Pain. Healing. And promise.

Today, my hope for you is to simply take one step. Take one step toward destruction, that terrifying unknown, in order to begin to see the promise on the other side. You may not see it right away, but, dear one, I promise you: it's there. And it's shimmering and brilliant and so much more than you could have ever dreamed up for yourself.

You are seen. You are known. You are braver than you're giving yourself credit for. And you are deeply, deeply connected.

Go forth, dear one. Stretch your wings. The darkness ain't got shit on you.

Love always,

Leilani

ABOUT THE AUTHOR

Leilani Mañulu is an Earth angel, shaman, and etheric translator, channeling messages from the Universe in service of guiding humanity toward our collective awakening. She is a queer, mixed-race, Filipino, cisgender woman of color, an Army brat who grew up (mostly) in Denver, Colorado and Lawton, Oklahoma.

Leilani is also the host of "The Intuitive Activist" podcast, where she unpacks spiritual truths with mediums, healers, and creatives from all walks of life in hopes of improving our world for generations to come.

Before she began writing and podcasting full-time, Leilani built her career as an HR leader and a social entrepreneur, empowering organizations to be more empathic, equitable, and human-centered. Leilani is a fierce racial and social justice activist, using her platform to regularly challenge systems of oppression and bring light to even the darkest of spaces.

Leilani lives in Seattle, Washington with her son James Finley and travels often, desiring to see as much of the world as humanly possible.

CPSIA information can be obtained
at www.ICGtesting.com
Printed in the USA
JSHW021918241022
32052JS00003B/11